Airplane Crashes

Titles in the Man-Made Disasters series include:

Airplane Crashes

Nuclear Accidents

Oil and Chemical Spills

Shipwrecks

Tragedies of Space Exploration

MAN-MADE
DISASTERS

Airplane Crashes

Gordon D. Laws and Lauren M. Laws

LUCENT
BOOKS®

THOMSON
————✦————™
GALE

San Diego • Detroit • New York • San Francisco • Cleveland • New Haven, Conn. • Waterville, Maine • London • Munich

© 2004 by Lucent Books. Lucent Books is an imprint of The Gale Group, Inc., a division of Thomson Learning, Inc.

Lucent Books® and Thomson Learning™ are trademarks used herein under license.

For more information, contact
Lucent Books
27500 Drake Rd.
Farmington Hills, MI 48331-3535
Or you can visit our Internet site at http://www.gale.com

LIBRARY OF CONGRESS CATALOGING-IN-PUBLICATION DATA

Laws, Gordon D.
  Airplane crashes / by Gordon D. Laws and Lauren M. Laws.
    p. cm. -- (Manmade disasters)
  Summary: Discusses safety issues, types of disasters, rescue methods, and investigations
    of airplane crashes, as well as exploring future safety procedures.
  Includes bibliographical references and index.
  ISBN 1-59018-054-2 (hardback : alk. paper)
  1. Aircraft accidents--Juvenile literature. I. Laws, Lauren M. II.
Title. III. Series.
  TL553.5.L335 2004
  363.12'465--dc21   2003005197

Printed in the United States of America

Contents

Foreword

In the late 1990s a University of Florida study came to a surprising conclusion. Researchers determined that the local residents they surveyed were more afraid of nuclear accidents, chemical spills, and other man-made disasters than they were of natural disasters such as hurricanes and floods. This finding seemed especially odd given that natural disasters are often much more devastating than man-made disasters, at least in terms of human lives. The collapse of the two World Trade Center towers on September 11, 2001, was among the worst human-caused disasters in recent memory, yet even its horrific death toll of roughly three thousand pales in comparison to, for example, the 1976 earthquake in China that killed an estimated seven hundred thousand people.

How then does one explain people's overarching fear of man-made disasters? One factor mentioned by the Florida researchers related to the widespread perception that natural hazards are "acts of God" that no one can control. Earthquakes, forest fires, and the like are thus accepted as inevitable. Man-made disasters are viewed differently, as unpredictable yet maddeningly preventable. Even worse, because these new technologies are so incredibly complex—a 747 airliner has 6 million parts, the one hundred-foot-long control room of a nuclear power plant has thousands of gauges and controls—the root cause of the disaster can often be shockingly trivial. One notorious 1972 airliner crash occurred when a tiny lightbulb, the indicator for whether the nose landing gear was down, burned out. While in flight, the captain, copilot, and engineer decided to replace the bulb. With the crew distracted, someone in the cockpit accidentally disengaged the autopilot and the plane flew into the ground, killing 98 of 176 onboard.

Man-made disasters are also distressing because they are so furtive in their deadliness. The hazardous radiation emitted by the nuclear accident at Tokaimura, Japan, in 1999 could neither be seen nor smelled, and the lethal gas that leaked from a Union Carbide pesticide factory in India in 1984 settled silently over the city of Bhopal, killing thousands in their homes.

Another factor may be the widespread perception that man-made disasters are worse than ever. This is probably true although faulty designs and shoddy workmanship have been causing building collapses, dam failures, and ship sinkings for thousands of years. Beginning with the twentieth century, what is new is industrial technology, such as nuclear power and oil refining, that can affect huge areas over many years when something goes wrong. The radiation from the disaster at the Chernobyl nuclear power plant in 1986 spread worldwide and has closed local areas to human habitation to this day. Finally, man-made disasters have begun to compound each other: In January 1997, a massive oil spill caused by the shipwreck of a Russian tanker in the Sea of Japan threatened to clog crucial cooling systems in nearby nuclear power plants.

Fortunately, humanity can learn vital lessons from man-made disasters. Practical insights mean that ocean liners no longer ply the seas, as the *Titanic* did, with too few lifeboats and no ability to see in the dark. Nuclear power plants are not being built with the type of tin-can containment building that Chernobyl had. The latest generation of oil tankers has double hulls, which should vastly reduce oil spills. On the more philosophical level man-made disasters offer valuable insights into issues relating to progress and technology, risk and safety, and government and corporate responsibility.

The Man-Made Disasters series presents a clear and up-to-date overview of such dramatic events as airplane crashes, nuclear accidents, oil and chemical spills, tragedies of space exploration, shipwrecks, and building collapses. Each book in the series serves as both a wide-ranging introduction and a guide to further study. Fully documented primary and secondary source quotes enliven the narrative. Sidebars highlight important events, personalities, and technologies. Annotated bibliographies provide readers with ideas for further research. Finally, the many facts and unforgettable stories relate the hubris—pride bordering on arrogance—as well as the resiliency of daring pioneers, bold innovators, brave rescuers, and lucky survivors.

Safety Is Relative

On September 17, 1908, less than five years after Orville and Wilbur Wright flew the first airplane at Kitty Hawk, North Carolina, the brothers brought their latest model to Fort Myer, Virginia, to demonstrate it to U.S. Army officials. The military was looking for a flying machine that could carry a passenger, attain forty miles per hour, and fly for at least one hour. Over the previous two weeks, Orville made a number of preliminary flights. Now he was to take up Lieutenant Thomas Selfridge, a member of the army board that was evaluating the plane and a pioneering aviator in his own right.

As Orville readied the plane, Selfridge waved to the enthusiastic crowd of more than two thousand spectators. Soon, Wright and Selfridge were off, and Orville flew along easily, minimizing his maneuvers to reduce any dangers. After three laps over the crowd at 150 feet, Orville heard the beginnings of trouble, tapping sounds he had not heard before. He thought he might shut off the engine and glide to a stop when he heard two loud thumps and saw something fly off the plane. It would later be determined that this was one of the two wooden propellers, which had split and then severed a rudder control wire. The accident left the plane unmanageable. As Orville related: "I continued to push the levers, when the machine suddenly turned to the left. I reversed the levers to stop the turning and to bring the wings on a level. Quick as a flash, the machine turned down in front and started straight for the ground."[1]

Orville turned off the engine and tried to glide, but the plane would not cooperate. To the horror of the crowd the plane plunged from a height of about one hundred feet and plowed into the ground. Orville broke his leg and several ribs. Selfridge was taken away unconscious and later died from a fractured skull. The investigation determined that the cracked propeller had been a new, and previously untested, design. Orville and Wilbur tinkered with the Wright Flyer to eliminate this and other flaws, and the military later accepted it as the world's first military aircraft, but the first fatality of modern aviation entered the history books.

Inherent Dangers

The plane crash that killed Selfridge was soon followed by others that claimed the lives of aviation pioneers. The co-founder of Rolls-Royce, Charles Stewart Rolls, for example, was killed on July 12, 1910, in Bournemouth, England, when his biplane crashed from an altitude of only twenty feet. Rolls was the first British flyer to die in a plane accident. On April 3, 1912, Calbraith Perry Rodgers, thirty-three, an American aviator who made the first transcontinental flight, became the first to die in a crash attributed to striking a bird when he was killed during an air show in Long Beach, California. Such highly publicized air crashes soon caused the public to wonder if air travel would ever be safe. Primitive airplane designs had few safety features, and many were often thought of only after crashes revealed fatal flaws.

▼ Army troops go to the aid of pilot Orville Wright and his mortally injured passenger Thomas Selfridge after their plane crashed.

Gradually, air travel has indeed gotten much safer. Statistically speaking, it is now one of the safest modes of transportation, especially compared to the annual death toll from automobile accidents. In the United States, in three out of the past ten years (1993, 1998, and 2002), the commercial airline industry experienced exactly zero accident-related fatalities. Even so, over that decade, in the United States approximately fourteen hundred passengers and crew were killed in twenty nine separate airliner accidents, including the four terrorist acts on September 11, 2001, that claimed 266 lives. These deaths occurred over some 160 million flight hours. Because most fatal airplane crashes occur during takeoffs and landings, however, the risk of flying is more dependent upon the number of connecting flights taken on any one trip, rather than the total time aloft or distance traveled.

Accident rates in the United States and Europe, moreover, are lower than in many other countries of the world. Although the United States had no fatalities in 2002, eleven major airline crashes worldwide collectively claimed about one thousand lives. Because planes have gotten bigger and are now capable of carrying more and more people, the accidents that do occur are often horrifying in scope. The February 19, 2003, crash of an Iranian military jetliner into snowcapped mountains took 302 lives, putting it among the ten worst crashes in history. The initial investigation suggested that bad weather and high winds contributed, though aviation officials say that Iran's Russian-built aircraft have been particularly susceptible to disasters.

Whatever the final findings in Iran, the investigation is likely to point to the need for new safety measures that could save future lives. As the number of planes aloft at any one time continues to increase every year, so also grows the possibility for deadly crashes and accidents.

CHAPTER ONE

Diverse Disasters

Being inside a plane as it goes down and crashes is a harrowing experience, one best understood through the testimonies of those who have survived. Passengers, crew, pilots, and even bystanders on the ground are often caught unaware, and the decisions they make in the few precious seconds before and after a crash can mean the difference between life and death—not only for themselves but for others around them.

The most spectacular crashes involve violent collisions in midair or sudden plunges from high altitudes to the earth, from which there are typically few or no survivors. Such crashes receive the greatest publicity, but they occur relatively infrequently. The vast majority of airplane crashes happen on or near the ground, and are survivable for at least some of the passengers and crew. Even so the experience is terrifying and unforgettable, something that will stay with them throughout their lives.

The Danger Zone: Takeoffs and Landings

A cliché among pilots is that flying is hours of boredom punctuated by two minutes of terror on each end. During takeoff of a fully loaded 747, the largest commercial airplane in the world, pilots rev the four highly tuned jet engines. From a standstill the seven hundred thousand-pound aircraft must achieve 180 miles per hour to lift into the sky before the end of a twelve thousand-foot runway. During landings, whether at night or during a storm, a 747 traveling at 160 miles per hour hits the runway with so much force its eighteen, four-foot-diameter tires must be filled with nitrogen at one hundred times the pressure of an ordinary car tire.

According to a recent scientific analysis of the relative safety of flying and driving, "A study carried out by Boeing indicates that out of 7,071 worldwide airline fatalities during the interval between 1991 and 2000, 95 percent happened either during takeoff and climb after takeoff, or during descent and landing. Conversely, only 5 percent of the fatalities resulted from accidents that occurred at cruising altitudes."[2] About half of all airliner accidents occur during the approach and landing phase of the flight, and about one-third are due to planes overrunning the end of the runway. During takeoffs and landings, planes can hydroplane on wet runways, slide on ice or snow, lose control from a tire blowout, experience strange forces from a previous plane's turbulent exhaust—the possibilities are numerous, with many having potentially deadly effects.

The stunning crash of a Concorde supersonic plane in Paris on July 25, 2000, illustrates the dangers. The high-tech Concorde is perhaps the most widely recognized commercial plane in the world. Able to cruise at twice the speed of sound, it cuts the usual seven-hour flying time across the Atlantic

▶ A Japanese businessman inside a nearby plane snapped this rare picture of Air France Flight 4590, with fire trailing from one of the Concorde's engines during takeoff.

Ocean in half. Soon after the first Concorde went into service in 1976, the result of a joint project of French and British state-supported companies, the fleet of thirteen sleek jets became the choice of the wealthy for transatlantic travel. By the turn of the millennium, a round-trip ticket was running more than $10,000, many times the cost on a regular airline.

Like more mundane planes, the Concorde is subject to the dangers involved with takeoffs and landings. On that fateful summer day in 2000, an Air France Concorde took off from Charles de Gaulle Airport near Paris, bound for New York. The takeoff for Flight 4590 seemed normal in the first few seconds, and communication with the control tower indicated no problem. But just moments into the takeoff, the copilot warned the pilot, "Watch out," and the control tower called a moment later, saying, "Concorde zero . . . 4590, you have flames (unclear) you have flames behind you."[3] After

▲ Eighteen of fifty-four passengers and crew members perished when an EgyptAir 737 crashed in foggy weather on its approach to Tunis Airport in May 2002.

struggling to raise the plane and retract the landing gear, the pilots lost control of the aircraft, and the Concorde plunged into a hotel outside the airport, killing all 109 people onboard and four people on the ground. Witnesses described flames spewing out of the Concorde's left side, and photos show a ribbon of flames trailing from the jet as it arched over the trees.

When Nothing Can Be Done

Most accidents happen on takeoffs and landings because that is when machine and operator face the greatest threats from weather and other factors. In the case of the Concorde, mechanical hazards within and without the aircraft were particularly to blame. The Concorde's tires were at a much higher pressure than typical airplane tires because they had to perform at much higher speeds. The higher pressure, however, made them more susceptible to bursting. Just before the Concorde had taken off, a Continental DC-10 had dropped a sixteen-inch piece of metal on the runway during its departure roll. No one noticed the metal and the Concorde hit it on takeoff, causing a tire to burst. Tire pieces pierced the Concorde's fuel tank and started the fire that brought down the plane. After the Concorde crash, tire manufacturer Michelin modified the Concorde tire to make it more puncture-proof and capable of functioning even when 40 percent deflated.

In the Concorde's case, the transcripts and flight information reveal a well-seasoned crew that handled the takeoff dangers as well as anybody possibly could. David Learmount, editor of *Flight International* magazine, told the BBC that the pilots and crew were blameless:

> They made no mistakes, and performed the drills appropriate to the information they had exactly as they had been drilled to do in training, and all without panic. When the aircraft crashed it was because it had become uncontrollable, and there was nothing that the crew could have done to prevent that situation arising. This is an accident in which the well-worn verdict "pilot error" will play no part whatsoever.[4]

Tragically, for the crew and passengers of the Concorde, the obstacles the plane faced were too great for any person to overcome. Loaded with fuel for the transatlantic flight, with

AN UNLUCKY SEVEN:
THE DEADLIEST CRASHES IN HISTORY

The following are the seven deadliest airplane crashes in history, by passenger deaths (thus excluding the coordinated attacks of September 11, 2001, in which most of the three thousand deaths were people on the ground).

1. On March 27, 1977, in Tenerife, Canary Islands, a KLM 747 collided with a Pan Am 747 on the runway during heavy fog, killing 583. Sixty-six on the Pan Am plane survived.

2. On August 12, 1985, in Japan, a Japan Airlines 747 experienced a mechanical failure that caused it to plow into a mountain, killing 520 people and sparing only four.

3. On November 12, 1996, near New Delhi, India, a Saudi Arabian 747 and a Kazakhstan Airlines Ilyushin-76 collided in midair just outside the city, killing all 349 people onboard both planes.

4. On March 3, 1974, outside Paris, a Turkish airliner lost a rear cargo door just after takeoff and crashed, killing 346.

5. On June 23, 1985, near the coast of Ireland, an Air India 747 plunged into the sea after a bomb blew up in the forward cargo section. All 329 onboard were killed.

6. On February 19, 2003, a military plane carrying 284 Iranian Revolutionary Guard soldiers and eighteen crew members crashed into a mountain in the middle of a snowstorm. All 302 were killed.

7. On August 19, 1980, in Riyadh, Saudi Arabia, a Lockheed L1011 performed a successful emergency landing just after takeoff because of a fire in a cargo area. But the crew was unable to open the emergency doors, and smoke and fire killed all 301 people on the plane.

both left wing engines out, the damaged Concorde could not gain the airspeed and altitude it needed to stay aloft. Despite all their training, the pilots did not have the best survivors' helper on their side: luck.

Nightmare in the Sky

While most airplane crashes occur during takeoffs and landings, accidents can also happen in midflight. In recent years near midair collisions have increased, primarily because of the growing traffic in the sky. In 1999 the Federal Aviation Administration (FAA) received more than 250 voluntary reports of near midair collisions, about thirty of which were

▲ A picture taken of the plane shows the stripped away section of forward fuselage that Aloha Flight 243 lost during mid-flight.

categorized as representing a "critical hazard." Actual midair collisions remain relatively rare, happening less frequently than engine burnouts and other examples of midair structural failures.

If a midair collision or structural failure is not immediately fatal for all involved, it can become a life-or-death test of a pilot's skill. An airplane that is failing in flight is a terrifying challenge, and even the best training cannot prepare a pilot for all the possible scenarios. Still, with the right mix of skill and luck, a pilot can be instrumental in saving lives. That was the case on April 28, 1988, as Aloha Flight 243, carrying eighty-nine passengers and six crew and industry members, was traveling from Hilo, Hawaii, to Honolulu.

The 737 had just reached its cruising altitude of twenty-four thousand feet when the pilot heard a crack and a whoosh and felt the plane depressurize—quickly lose its supply of air. The portion of the fuselage covering the first-class cabin had ripped off, and a flight attendant in the aisle was sucked out into the sky, never to be seen again. Captain Robert

Schornstheimer and copilot Madeline Tompkins immediately donned their oxygen masks and rapidly descended toward Maui, using hand signals to communicate because of the tremendous wind noise.

While the fuselage caused the main problems, other parts of the plane began to fail. The pilots later reported that the controls had felt loose and not entirely responsive. As Schornstheimer slowed the plane's airspeed, the plane became less manageable. When he tried to communicate with the flight attendants, he got no response. At eleven thousand feet, there was sufficient oxygen to breathe, so all removed their masks. Near the airport, Schornstheimer lowered the normal landing gear, although the nose gear failed. He tried the manual controls for the nose gear, but his instruments did not say whether the gear had worked. Finally, as he began the landing approach, he determined that one of the plane's two engines had failed. The plane rocked, and the ride in was jumpy. Even so, Schornstheimer managed to make a safe landing. Only the flight attendant sucked from the plane was lost—there was one severe injury and a handful of minor injuries, but all other passengers survived without harm.

The pilots' successful handling of the accident was dramatized in the made-for-TV movie *Miracle Landing,* and many passengers credited Schornstheimer and Tompkins for their skill in saving their lives. Even so, the two pilots could not deny the role of luck in surviving the accident. After the initial disintegration, the plane mostly held together under great duress, and the pilots were close to an airport where they could make a safe landing and get needed help.

The root cause of this crash—metal of the fuselage had grown weak over the thousands of flights the plane had made—points to an issue that is becoming increasingly worrisome as airlines try to survive tough economic times. Keeping an aging fleet of airliners aloft can be a financial and maintenance challenge. When it took off on its final flight, the Aloha 737 was nineteen years old, which is not terribly old for an aircraft. But it had completed almost ninety thousand "flight cycles" (one takeoff and landing), which was the second highest number among all the 737s active worldwide.

The Rescue of Flight 232

Accidents that cause a pilot to lose almost all control of the plane can be even more harrowing than the type of fuselage failure Aloha 243 experienced. Such was the case in the series of failures Captain Al Haynes faced when a DC-10 he was piloting plunged from thirty-seven thousand feet. Haynes, a former naval pilot and veteran of United Airlines for thirty-five years at the time of the crash, placed much of the credit on a pilot's best friend in a disaster—luck. He added that four other factors were crucial in reducing the scope of the disaster: communications, preparation, execution, and cooperation.

Flight 232 departed Denver in the early afternoon of July 19, 1989, and headed for Philadelphia. An hour into the flight, an explosion suddenly rocked the rear of the plane, the site of

▼ A mechanical failure led to the crash of Flight 232 in Sioux City, Iowa, in July 1989.

the DC-10's center engine. (Two additional engines are under the wings.) The engine malfunction shot pieces of shrapnel into vital aircraft control components, disabling the craft's entire hydraulic system.

Like most modern planes, DC-10s rely on hydraulic lines to control everything from the rudder for steering to the elevators (a movable part of the horizontal tail wing) for controlling pitch—angle up and down. Hydraulic lines depend upon a fluid pushed by pumps to exert force. Because losing hydraulic pressure could be so disastrous, planes have many backups, or redundancies, built into the system. DC-10s, for example, have three completely independent hydraulic systems, with two engine-driven pumps per system. Each system has its own fluid reservoir and supply and return lines. Haynes would later estimate that enough redundancy was built into the system to put the odds of a complete hydraulic failure at about 1 billion to one. In other words, Haynes says, the system was considered to be failsafe. Yet on that day in July 1989 the unthinkable happened:

> Murphy's Law caught up with the airline industry and our aircraft lost all three hydraulic systems. That left us at 37,000 feet with no ailerons to control roll, no rudders to co-ordinate a turn, no elevators to control pitch, no leading edge devices to help us slow down for landing, no trailing edge flaps to be used in landing, no spoilers on the wings to slow us down in flight or to help braking on the ground, no nosewheel steering and no brakes. That did not leave us a great deal to work with.[5]

Luck and Tragedy

Air traffic control personnel directed the falling plane to Sioux City, Iowa, as Haynes, the crew, and an off-duty airman struggled to cope. They had to try to steer the plane by manipulating the amount of throttle given to either of the still-functioning engines on each side of the plane. Haynes said, "By adding thrust on one side and reducing thrust on another we could force the aircraft in a skid to turn one way or another." Gradually they managed to direct the plane toward a landing strip at Sioux City. According to Haynes, their biggest problem was the lack of ability to control the plane's angle of descent. "With no pitch control, and just the slight amount of substitute steering capability we had, it is a wonder to me that we ever got the aircraft on the ground,"[6] he said.

After forty-five agonizing minutes in the barely controlled plane, Haynes and his crew neared the Sioux City airport. Three hundred feet above the ground, the plane pitched downward. It hit the ground unevenly, remarkably enough on a runway. The 737 bounced and broke apart, spewing fuel and fire across the ground, killing 110 passengers and one crew member. Even so, 175 passengers survived, as did ten crew members, including Haynes and three others in the cockpit.

"The things that we happened to try that day (not having any idea of what would result because this situation had not been expected or practiced for)," Haynes related, "happened to be the right things, and they happened to work. So luck played a very big part in even getting the aircraft to respond."[7]

▶ An NTSB investigator looks for clues in the broken-open passenger compartment of Flight 232 two days after the plane's crash landing.

Haynes and his crew were honored by the airline industry with special commendations for extraordinary professionalism and valour.

The good fortune of those who managed to survive Flight 232 was offset by the tragedy of those passengers who died from the impact or from the fire started by the spilled fuel. All too frequently, plane passengers who survive impact with the ground or water face another dire challenge: getting out of the wreckage before losing their lives to fire or smoke.

Fire in the Cabin

Plane disasters often start with a loud bang or a sudden dive, like those experienced on Aloha 243 and United Airlines 232. The initial shock can quickly give way to panic and chaos, especially in accidents that happen on takeoff and landing where the crash happens quickly. Statistics show that 60 percent of all plane disasters involve fire, and the survivability of a cabin can be less than two minutes once a fire is raging. With such forces against them, crew members and passengers must work together quickly.

With a fire raging, time is short, as film director Barry Sonnenfeld (*Men in Black*) knows. Sonnenfeld is a reluctant air traveler, saying wryly, "The quote I give people is that every time I get off a plane, I view it as a failed suicide attempt."[8] Sonnenfeld's dark humor was reinforced when the Grumman executive jet he was aboard on February 16, 1999, ran off the end of a runway in Van Nuys, California. The jet crashed into several other airplanes on the ground and caught fire. Initially, crew members were unaware of the fire, and they tried to get all onboard out through the cockpit door. But Sonnenfeld noticed fuel spilling over the wing and fire raging, and when he pointed it out to the crew, they all exited out the back, jumping into the arms of waiting firefighters.

Sonnenfeld's experience fortunately involved no deaths or serious injuries. Passengers and crew had time to assess the situation and avoid tragedy. Many other incidents of fires on planes have resulted in far greater panic and disastrous outcomes. On February 1, 1991, a USAir 737 coming in for a landing at Los Angeles International Airport collided with a smaller SkyWest commuter aircraft. With the larger plane virtually on top of the smaller, the two aircraft slid together across the runway and slammed into, ironically, an abandoned fire station, where they caught fire. All twelve onboard the commuter plane died, while sixty-three passengers and four crew members aboard the USAir flight got out safely (thirty were injured, thirteen severely). But twenty passengers and two crew members onboard the USAir flight perished, and federal aviation officials concluded that eleven of those died on their way to an exit, overcome by toxic fumes from the fires.

Toxic gases released during a plane fire can be as deadly as the flames. Gases from burning fuel and airplane parts can include such hazards as carbon monoxide, hydrogen cyanide, hydrogen fluoride, and hydrogen chloride. Particles from the burning of cabin materials can also be hazardous to breathe. Toxic gases can knock people unconscious, and they can cause permanent damage in survivors. The oxygen masks provided by airlines cannot protect against them because the masks allow passengers to breathe air in the cabin as well as that coming through the tubes.

Panic on the Ground

Passengers who manage to survive the fires and other hazards inside the cabin of a downed airplane face ongoing dangers as they exit the craft and reach the ground. The chaos and confusion of the debris field, as well as potential ground fires, can harm survivors and rescuers alike. In one particularly tragic episode, on August 22, 1985, at Manchester International Airport in England, fifty-five people died without the plane ever getting airborne. The circumstances of the Manchester crash allowed it to become a benchmark case in managing rescues and fighting fires.

The pilots of the British Airtours 737 were preparing for a routine early morning flight to the Greek island of Corfu. The plane was packed with 130 passengers, mostly British tourists. Things began to go wrong on the takeoff roll. The pilots heard a muffled explosion, and thinking a tire had blown they aborted the takeoff. Actually an engine had failed and fuel had caught on fire. When the plane slowed to a stop, burning fuel spilled onto the runway under the plane. Flames also moved quickly from the left wing to the rear of

the craft, where they penetrated the passenger cabin and engulfed two exits.

The first emergency door that crew members went to failed to open. Heat and fumes caused panic as passengers rushed toward the front of the plane and got wedged into the narrow aisle. A crew member returned to the first door and dislodged it just as firefighters began spraying foam on the plane. The slide was put in place but panic, smoke, and confusion prevailed among passengers. People started plunging out the exit door but one man got stuck in it. A boy hoisted over the man was the last rescued passenger to survive. Thick, black smoke overwhelmed two flight attendants who had been directing traffic near the rear of the aircraft. Neither they nor anyone else escaped through the rear.

Seven minutes after the plane had rolled to a halt on the runway, firefighters entered the aircraft in search of those overcome by fumes. An explosion blew one firefighter out of the aircraft, however, forcing rescuers to withdraw until more water could be brought in. The tail of the aircraft also broke off during the rescue effort, adding to the chaos on the

▲ In 1991 thirty-four people died from a runway collision and ensuing fire at Los Angeles International Airport.

THE WORST SINGLE-PLANE DISASTER

Few crashes have been as horrific or as full of dangers in the plane and on the ground as the one that happened to Japan Airlines Flight 123 on August 12, 1985. The 747, out of Tokyo and bound for Osaka, had been modified to hold more passengers and was full. Shortly after takeoff, it experienced a serious malfunction in the rear tail section, rendering all controls useless. The problem was eventually traced to an improper repair Boeing had made years earlier. The flight lumbered along with the pilots wrestling for control and warning passengers to stay seated. Suddenly it slammed high into the side of Mount Osutaka. A flyover revealed at least ten fires burning among the sprawling wreckage, likely taking the lives of many who might have been spared. Further, the plane wreckage seemed to have slipped down the mountain, worsening the situation for any possible survivors. Doctors later concluded that a number of the victims had actually survived impact but had died from shock and exposure to the sub-freezing temperatures on the mountain. Apparently some of the 520 victims could have been saved had rescuers arrived more quickly.

ground and in the plane. In the end, fifty-three passengers and two crew members died. Forty-five of these victims died not from burns but from inhaling smoke and toxic gases such as carbon monoxide and hydrogen cyanide.

Even removing survivors and injured persons from the wreckage area can be a challenge. Passengers are often dazed and rattled, and the dangers of smoke, fire, and debris on the ground are often not clear to them. The Manchester crash highlighted the need for additional precautions on the ground for rescuing dazed and shocked survivors.

The Plunge into the Sea

The chaos and danger of a crash are magnified when one occurs at sea. Planes crashing into water are even more lethal than those hitting ground because, in addition to the dangers of impact, fire, and smoke, survivors can drown if rescuers are remote. Cold water and tossing seas make rescue even less likely. Even so, crash victims have been known to survive by clinging to floating seat cushions, pieces of the fuselage, or even luggage.

Some 179 people faced this grim scene on January 30, 2000, when a Kenya Airways Airbus A310, a twin-engine commercial jet with a capacity of about 280, crashed into the Atlantic Ocean shortly after takeoff from Abidjan, Ivory Coast. The plane experienced a false alarm about a stalled engine. This caused the pilot to take unnecessary emergency actions and ultimately to fly the plane into the sea. The plane burst into flames and broke apart as it hit the water, scattering debris. A fuel fire raged on top of the water for thirty minutes before dying down.

Samuel Ogbada Adje, one of the ten survivors, managed to swim a thousand yards through the cold waters of the Atlantic to shore. In an interview he said the plane "wasn't quite balanced, and the next thing we knew we were in the water." Adje complained that the rescue could have been far more successful (nine other passengers survived by clinging to pieces of the wreckage). "If they had come sooner," he said, "a lot of us would have been saved. We waited two hours for people to rescue us."[9]

Rescue efforts for the Kenya Airways flight were hampered by both the watery scene and a lack of equipment. Many of the survivors were pulled from the sea by volunteers who arrived in private boats. If the plane had gone down farther out in the ocean, it is likely even fewer would have survived.

Coming Down in a Community

While ocean crashes might be the most perilous for passengers and crew members, the difficulties of ground collisions are magnified when an airplane comes down in a neighborhood. Chances of survival on the plane are far fewer, as the aircraft collides with ground structures and causes explosions and building collapses. In 2001, the 525 passengers and crew killed in major U.S. carrier disasters were dwarfed by the three thousand deaths on the ground caused by the three terrorist-piloted jets that struck the two World Trade Center towers and the Pentagon on September 11. Excluding these horrific acts, however, only six people died on the ground from the other three fatal airline crashes that occurred during 2001 in the United States.

All six of these fatalities occurred in the Rockaway section of Queens, New York. On November 12, 2001, a day off for many because of Veterans' Day, American Airlines Flight 587 lost a tailfin and rudder and subsequently crashed in the city neighborhood, killing all 255 onboard. The crash was devastating for a neighborhood that had lost friends and family members, including a number of firemen, in the September 11 terrorist attacks.

As the crash occurred, the scene on the ground was terrifying for residents. Many children were home from school for the Veterans' Day holiday, and several survived the disaster by mere feet. Kevin McKeon was having coffee in his home's kitchen with his wife, Eileen, and their young daughter when the plane crashed. "The next thing we know, we felt this shudder and the room just exploded," Kevin said. "My daughter got blown through the patio doors. My wife got blown into the living room. And I got blown out the patio doors behind my

▼ Almost half the passengers onboard this twin-prop plane were rescued, as it plunged into the Philippines' Manila Bay not far from land.

daughter."[10] In McKeon's case, one of the engines had dropped into his yard, crushing the family boat and setting the house on fire.

The Queens crash caused additional problems for rescuers, as dozens of fires in the neighborhood erupted, caused by falling parts as the plane broke apart.

▲ New York City firefighters search through the rubble of American Airlines Flight 587, which claimed the lives of 261 people.

Midair and Runway Collisions

Crashes in neighborhoods heighten the possibilities of tremendous losses of life. But few crashes compare in enormity to midair and runway collisions. Though occurring rarely, midair and runway collisions are doubly costly in human life—survival rates are very low, and the combined passenger totals bring extensive human devastation. Two of the three most deadly crashes in history involved colliding planes: the famous Canary Islands runway collision in March 1977 between two Boeing 747s, which killed 583 people, and a midair collision in November 1996 between a cargo plane and a 747 near New Delhi, India, which killed 349.

The Canary Islands collision was an indirect and tragic consequence of terrorism. A small bomb planted by a terrorist exploded in a terminal in the Las Palmas, Canary Islands, airport. The airport was closed for investigation, and traffic was diverted to Tenerife, another of the small Spanish islands off the coast of North Africa. Rain and fog blanketed the Canary Islands, obscuring runway markers. KLM Flight 4805 with 234 passengers and 14 crew members had been cleared to take off, while Pan Am Flight 1736 had been given instructions on its takeoff runway. Apparently disoriented by the fog, the pilot put the plane in the path of the KLM flight just as it was accelerating for takeoff. The KLM pilot tried desperately to get the plane off the ground, while the Pan Am pilot tried to move the plane onto the grass. Even so, the KLM tail

▼ In a dramatic city crash, the tail of a massive Russian cargo plane came to rest against an apartment building on December 7, 1997.

FAMOUS VICTIMS OF AIRPLANE CRASHES

Politicians, entertainers, and athletes are premier frequent flyers. Perhaps not surprisingly many such prominent people have lost their lives in airplane crashes, including legendary Notre Dame football coach Knute Rockne in 1931, actress Carole Lombard in 1942, baseball player Roberto Clemente in 1972, country singer John Denver in 1997, and Minnesota senator Paul Wellstone in 2002.

Another particularly tragic crash occurred on February 3, 1959. Rock star Buddy Holly was just 22 when the Beechcraft Bonanza he was riding in went down in a winter storm near Clear Lake, Iowa. Also killed were the Big Bopper (J.P. Richardson, 29), the hit singer of "Chantilly Lace," budding Mexican American singer Ritchie Valens, 17, and the pilot, Roger Peterson.

One of the most highly publicized crashes in recent years claimed the lives of John F. Kennedy Jr., 38, son of the late president John F. Kennedy; John Jr.'s wife, Carolyn Bessette Kennedy, 35; and her older sister, Lauren Bessette, 37. On July 16, 1999, the Piper Saratoga Kennedy was piloting plunged into the ocean near Martha's Vineyard. Kennedy was an inexperienced pilot with a recently injured foot flying by instruments in a twilight haze over the ocean.

clipped the Pan Am plane. The KLM plane got into the air, but made it only one hundred feet before it lost control and crashed, killing all onboard. The Pan Am aircraft broke into pieces and caught fire. Nine of the 16 crew members were killed, and only 52 passengers out of 314 survived.

In the New Delhi incident, the collision occurred in midair, as a Saudi Arabian 747 was taking off and a Kazakhstan Airlines Ilyushin-76 was attempting to land. The collision ignited twin fireballs that lit up the sky and scattered airplane debris, baggage, and bodies over six miles of wheat and mustard fields. There were no survivors among the 312 passengers and crew aboard the 747 or the 37 aboard the Ilyushin-76. The collision occurred at an altitude of thirteen thousand feet, about seven minutes after the Saudi Arabian flight lifted off. It was blamed in part, on a lack of collision avoidance technology in the Kazakh plane.

Today, collision avoidance technology has become standard on most airplanes in industrialized countries. The systems typically alert pilots about imminent threats, plot the locations and angles of approach of nearby aircraft, and advise the pilot on evasive maneuvers.

On the Scene at the Rescue

The process of rescuing people from a plane crash begins as soon as warning is received that there are problems with a plane. Fast-acting rescue squads are often standing by when a plane goes down, but in other instances, crash sites are hard to reach and the challenge for rescuers is great. Though rescue procedures and technologies have improved over the years, the process can be chaotic, disheartening, and tragic. Even so, survivors hail their rescuers as heroes.

CHAPTER TWO

The Rescue

News stories about airplane accidents are common in the media, with articles that feature multiple fatalities leading the way. Human tragedies are a legitimate public concern, and the media is happy to provide the details. But surviving an air accident is far more common than media reports might lead one to believe. In the United States, about 95 percent of the passengers and crew who were involved in the more than 650 major carrier accidents that occurred from 1983 to 2002 survived. Some 55 percent survived in "serious" accidents (those involving heavy structural damage and life-threatening conditions). Throughout the world, the survival rate of an airplane accident is 90 percent.

In part, these findings reflect the diversity of accidents—from planes that skid more or less harmlessly off the runway on landing to planes that crash head-on into a mountain. Obviously, lower-impact crashes generally increase passengers' chances for survival. But even in the worst apparent disasters, a few people may survive, and emergency teams around the world have become adept at handling rescue missions. The Philippine coast guard was hailed, for example, for its timely work in the aftermath of a November 11, 2002, crash that occurred in Manila Bay. A Fokker 27, a twin-propeller, midsized craft, plunged into the water shortly after takeoff with thirty-four people aboard. Divers and rescue personnel were able to save sixteen of the passengers and crew.

A Crash Drill Turned Real

Communications are the first key to a successful rescue. The sooner airport and emergency response authorities know where an accident may happen, the sooner they can rush rescue workers to the area. Obviously, many crashes do not allow

▶ Despite the best efforts of rescue divers, eighteen of thirty-four passengers and crew were killed when a Fokker prop plane plunged into Manila Bay on November 11, 2002.

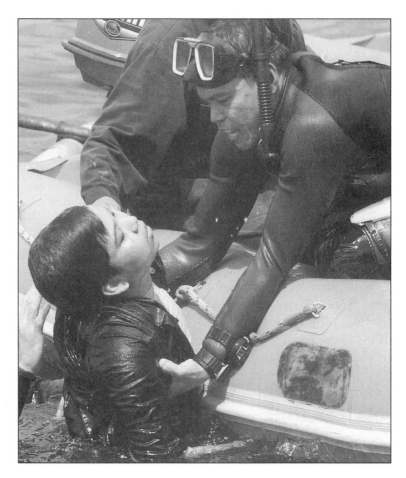

much notice or preparation time, but those that do have a far greater chance of producing survivors.

On that memorable day in August 1989, pilot Al Haynes knew his United Flight 232 was in trouble as it approached the Sioux City airport. When the malfunctions first developed, he and his copilots wrestled with the plane and struggled for solutions. They even radioed the San Francisco aero maintenance unit to consult with expert DC-10 mechanics. (The experts were as shocked as the pilots by the multiple hydraulic failures, and could offer no useful suggestions.) Meanwhile, the control tower in Chicago radioed local emergency workers who filled a plane with supplies and flew it to Sioux City so that it arrived just after the plane crash-landed.

Further, Haynes had crucial communications with the Sioux City control tower that helped plot where the plane would come down and where emergency supplies and workers should be placed. Haynes radioed the Sioux City tower, detailing all the control problems he was having, then offered his gloomy evaluation of landing the plane safely: "I have serious doubts about making the airport. Have you got someplace near there, that we might be able to ditch? Unless we get control of this airplane, we're going to put it down wherever it happens to be."[11]

Fortunately for Haynes and the survivors of Flight 232, Sioux City was prepared with supplies coming in from Chicago and with its own rescue services, and the flight controllers in the tower were able to help. They called local emergency services and radioed firefighter and first-response units to be prepared. Moments later, they radioed Haynes with good news: Emergency equipment near the projected landing area at the airport was standing by.

When Haynes expressed further doubt that he would be able to get the plane down at the airport, the tower radioed local emergency authorities in surrounding communities. These local officials dispatched emergency teams to visually spot the plane and follow it in case it came down in a field or near a suburban area. In further good luck for Haynes and the passengers, the airport had just been through airplane disaster drills, and they were prepared for what happened next.

A Disaster Reduced

Because seconds on the ground are crucial in saving lives, rescue workers improve the chances of helping survivors by being well-trained and well-positioned immediately before or after a crash. In the case of Aloha Flight 243, the Maui control tower alerted firefighter and rescue crews through a newly established emergency hotline and had them positioned alongside the runway well before the plane arrived. This effort reduced the risk of fire and enabled rescuers to get the injured off the plane quickly.

For Flight 232, the plane's ultimate landing spot was almost a miracle itself. When Haynes realized where he was headed, he notified the control tower that he was two minutes away. Unfortunately, the erratic nature of the plane's movement caught the tower temporarily off guard—they had stationed emergency personnel on a closed runway which, it

PREPARING FOR THE WORST

United Flight 232 benefited greatly from well-trained rescue personnel on the ground who had practiced airplane disaster situations. Across the United States, airplane disaster simulations happen at airports in accordance with FAA regulations. Personnel are required to stage full-scale air disaster drills that include a downed plane, fatalities, fire, and injured personnel. Firefighters, paramedics, doctors, nurses, hospitals, and numerous other disaster specialists are among those involved in such efforts.

Emergency planners are constantly finding new ways to prepare for worst-case scenarios. A recent drill at the Miramar Marine Corps air station, near San Diego, California, run by the military in cooperation with local emergency personnel, simulated the crash of a military transport KC-130 into a small building. The plane was then said to have come to a stop on the tarmac and exploded, killing and wounding at least seventy-eight people. The military began the rescue, but civilian ambulances, doctors, and firefighters also participated. Raul Velasco, a civilian emergency medical technician, told *North County Times* reporter Gidget Fuentes that in normal training situations, "You're looking at 15 to 20 patients. Here, you're working at an incident with a lot of people. It's a better opportunity [to test skills]." Many pilots and others credit such drills with saving lives when disasters actually occur.

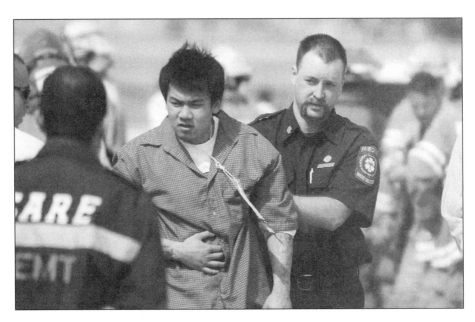

▲ Emergency personnel direct a "victim volunteer" to safety during a disaster drill held at Southern California's John Wayne Airport in March 2002.

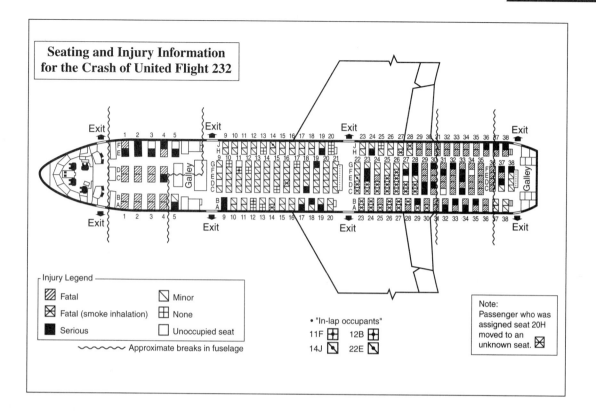

Seating and Injury Information
for the Crash of United Flight 232

Injury Legend

▨ Fatal	◻ Minor
⊠ Fatal (smoke inhalation)	⊞ None
■ Serious	☐ Unoccupied seat
∿∿∿ Approximate breaks in fuselage	

• "In-lap occupants"

11F ⊞   12B ⊞

14J ◻   22E ◻

Note:
Passenger who was
assigned seat 20H
moved to an
unknown seat. ⊠

turned out, Flight 232 was now headed for. With only minutes
to spare, rescue crews scrambled to clear the area. Haynes
managed to crash-land his plane in almost the exact spot
where the emergency drills had been practiced. Just as the
plane was about to touch down, rescue crews were able to fi-
nalize its position and notify the hospitals that the wounded
would soon be en route. One of the ground workers called the
other rescuers, saying, "I'm going to go ahead and go en route
out there to the command post. Let me advise anything that
you need, I'll have the comm center go ahead and notify
emergency hospitals and also the ambulances."[12]

Rescue teams and firefighters swarmed over the site, aid-
ing in getting people out of the wreck and offering emergency
medical treatment. Haynes and others in the cockpit were
trapped in the plane's nose, which had broken off from the
first-class cabin. Rescuers could not pull Haynes and the others free even using the "jaws of life," heavy-duty metal-cutting
instruments often used to extract car accident victims. Ultimately, Haynes says, "They came up with the idea to bring a
fork-lift over, and run the chains, the heavy chains . . . straight
down, and lift the cockpit straight up. And by doing this [they]

raised the cockpit [just high enough], and pulled us all out of the bottom. That's how they got us out of the airplane."[13]

The other survivors also experienced harrowing moments. Haynes writes in a separate essay:

> When they [the survivors] finally got out of the aircraft, they found themselves standing in a corn field, surrounded by corn eight feet high. . . . But they stayed calm and they helped each other. One of the survivors started climbing out of the aircraft and heard a baby crying; he went back inside, found the baby in an overhead bin where she had been tossed, took her out of the aircraft and brought her to her family that had been driven out by the thick smoke.[14]

▼ Flight 232 pilot Al Haynes, far left, takes questions at a press conference on July 19, 1990, held in conjunction with the commemoration of the crash one year earlier.

Mobilizing Doctors and Others

Getting the rescue teams to an airplane crash site is only a small part of the overall rescue operation. In general, rescue

planners prepare for different levels of disasters. The higher the level, the more rescuers, ambulances, doctors, and hospitals are involved. Live drills are held every three years, and so-called paper drills, revisions to the plans and procedural updates, are done each year.

At Sioux City, the planners had prepared with live drills just two years earlier and then had subsequently regularly updated their plans. Before the plane crashed, planners sent out a "level three" alert, indicating that a crash had already occurred. This mobilized not only rescue personnel, who moved more quickly to the scene, but also the hospital personnel who would need to prepare for a massive influx of wounded people. The timing was excellent: The hospitals at that time were going through their midafternoon shift change, and rather than send any doctors home, administrators kept all doctors on the floors waiting for arrivals.

In the meantime, the level three alert mobilized the National Guard in Des Moines, Iowa. They put together rescue and recovery materials and equipment and sent a flight to the airport that arrived shortly after Flight 232. Health specialists adept at handling posttraumatic stress disorder were also dispatched to the scene. These specialists began working with survivors as they were loaded into ambulances, and they continued their work at the hospitals. Because posttraumatic stress disorder can last for years, workers arranged with survivors to meet regularly after the crash to help manage their transition back to normal life.

When the plane finally hit the ground, the emergency personnel were ready. Ambulances made multiple runs between the scene and two local hospitals. Individual groups made up of a doctor, medical technician, and nurse met ambulances as they pulled up, and as soon as one team hustled a survivor off, another team stepped into its place.

▲ A Sioux City memorial to victims of United Airlines Flight 232 captures the spirit of the rescue effort.

Doctors from all specialties were summoned to the waiting areas so there would be sufficient medical help to attend those in need.

In the end, many lives on Flight 232 were spared, but 112 were also lost, and the memory has haunted survivors for years since then. Many have experienced survivor guilt, the feeling that they did not deserve to live when others had died and were just as deserving of rescue. Nevertheless, survivors are thankful for the highly skilled rescue and medical personnel who came to their aid at such a traumatic time.

Saved by Lobstermen

If a rescue could be ideal, it might be like that for Aloha Flight 243 or United Flight 232, where emergency crews are notified

▼ The crash of a twin-engine plane into a sheet metal plant in Leominster, Massachusetts, in April 2003 prompted the mobilization of firefighters, doctors, and other emergency personnel.

MANAGING FRAGILE PSYCHES

Traumatic incidents like airplane disasters can have profound effects on survivors' psyches. Certainly no survivor forgets the harrowing experience. Although a few report no subsequent fear of flying whatsoever, most have to contend with at least mild to moderate anxiety about flying. Nightmares are not uncommon, sometimes within the first few days after the crash. Vivid flashbacks of the event, in which survivors visualize themselves in the crash again and again, can happen suddenly and be triggered by seemingly insignificant incidents during the course of the day. Others suffer severe stress, or post-traumatic stress disorder (PTSD).

Severe stress can have powerful effects on people's relationships, marriages, and ability to function in normal activities. PTSD sufferers may withdraw from family members and may experience heightened states of arousal, periods when they become angry without reason and when they react suddenly in fear to normal noises or daily events.

Psychological treatment for airplane crash survivors can go on for years and can involve a mixture of therapy and medication. Many survivors confront their fear of the event by repeatedly talking through the incident with a trusted therapist until the details become less terrifying to contemplate. Others go through behavioral therapy in which they confront the reminders of the incident and manage their reactions and emotions. The overall process can be lengthy and painful for both survivors and their family members.

of the incident ahead of time, they have prepared themselves in advance with a plan, and they are ready to execute the plan. But plane crashes happen among all types of planes, in all types of terrain, and under all kinds of conditions. When a small plane crashes in a remote area, simply finding the site is the first challenge. Small planes that go down over water, like the one carrying John F. Kennedy Jr., his wife, and her sister, in July 1999, often yield no survivors. The particular circumstances of a small crash, however, ultimately determine the success of a rescue.

Such was the case of a fortunate pilot who plummeted into the ocean off the coast of New Hampshire. On July 11, 1952, Wallace Barnes of Connecticut was piloting a single-engine, four-person seaplane from Hartford, Connecticut, to Bar Harbor, Maine. (Seaplanes can land and take off on water, staying afloat either on watertight pontoons attached by struts to the fuselage, or on the fuselage itself.) Flying over the Atlantic, Barnes's plane developed engine trouble. When the engine finally conked out his plane fell from the sky and crash-landed into the water near Portsmouth, New Hampshire. To save his plane and his own life, Barnes threw his anchor out, hoping to steady the plane until help could come. But choppy waves and swift currents overwhelmed the plane and its anchor, and Barnes was swept toward the beach. Jagged rocks there would imperil the plane and expose Barnes to the ocean's cold water and dangerous currents.

Fortunately for Barnes, he happened to crash near two lobstermen, Arthur Moore and Carl Gray, who were pulling up traps. When the plane crashed, the two men sped their boat toward Barnes. They arrived when Barnes's craft was within fifteen feet of being smashed up against the rocks. Moore and Gray attached a line to the plane and towed it into deeper waters, where they got Barnes safely off the plane and onto the boat.

Meanwhile, additional help was on the way. The plane hit the water within view of Ely Plotkin's beachfront home. Plotkin witnessed the crash and reported the downed plane to the Portsmouth Harbor lifeboat station. Officers there sent out a Coast Guard spotter plane, which soon ran across the lobster boat hauling the downed plane. The plane directed two Coast Guard rescue boats to the site. One of the Coast Guard boats attached a line to the plane and hauled it to nearby New Castle. In the end, Barnes survived his crash into the treacherous Atlantic with only minor injuries. Fortunately for him, he had come down at just the right time and in the right place.

A Difficult Mountain Rescue

As in the case of Barnes, where menacing seas threatened the rescue, rescuers often face particularly challenging circumstances when planes crash. Some of the perils of rescue work come from the rugged terrain where planes crash. Remote locations coupled with bad weather can keep rescue crews from arriving in time to help survivors. It takes brave rescuers to face these dangers, and in some cases, even the best efforts are not enough.

While critics have said that rescuers did not do enough to save the victims of Japan Airlines Flight 123, others have pointed out the terrible odds they were up against. The wreckage was scattered on the high slopes of Mount Osutaka at night, which was just the beginning of rescuers' problems. Heavy clouds and stormy weather plagued the first rescue parties. Temperatures hovered around freezing, though summer conditions reigned below in the valleys. Even worse, the crash site was well beyond the reach of hiking trails, meaning that rescuers would have to battle against the rain and cold on unbroken terrain. A helicopter pilot that flew over the site shortly after the crash doubted that there could be any survivors and noted that there was no way for any rescue aircraft to land in the area. The U.S. military offered immediate assistance, but Japanese authorities declined.

Rescuers on the ground spent most of the night setting up a base in a mountain village in preparation for a recovery

▼ Japanese rescue teams search for survivors after the catastrophic 1985 crash of a fully loaded 747.

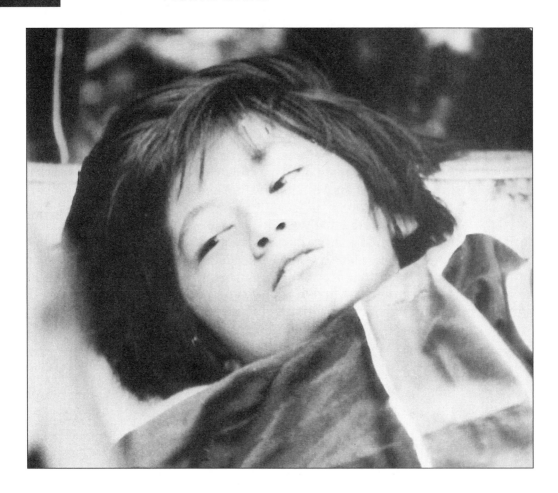

▲ Twelve-year-old Keiko Kawakami, one of only four survivors of Japan Airlines Flight 123, lies on a stretcher following her dramatic rescue some seventeen hours after the crash that killed 520 people.

mission the next day. Others started up the mountain, but the rain and mist slowed progress. The first rescuers finally arrived at the site around 9:00 A.M., fifteen hours after the crash. Later in the morning, when daylight brightened the area and the fog lifted, army paratroopers rappelled in from helicopters. The rescuers were surprised to find four survivors: a mother and her eight-year-old daughter, a twelve-year-old girl with mere bumps and bruises, and a flight attendant pinned in the wreckage with a broken pelvis. All had been seated in the rear of the plane, which had broken off from the main body and come to rest in a small valley without catching fire.

Yumi Ochiai, the flight attendant who survived, recalled the horror of the crash and the long wait for rescuers battling the elements. She said of the crashlanding, "Finally, when all the noise and confusion of impact had stopped, I was able to unfasten my seatbelt. But then I found I was trapped between the seats and couldn't move at all." Even worse, a report of the accident records, "Somewhere amongst the wreckage around her, she could hear children crying. Their cries were quite loud at first, but gradually they became weaker and weaker, and finally there was only silence. After night fell she heard the sound of a helicopter overhead, but it went away and she lapsed into sleep."[15]

A Remote Small Plane Crash

More than five hundred small planes crashed in the United States in 2001. Like large crashes, small crashes can happen in hard-to-reach areas—swamps, mountains, and oceans. Pinpointing the site of an accident can be more challenging, with less wreckage and fewer people to spot. But some of the most dramatic rescues have received little notice because they involved few passengers. At least one of these illustrates not only the hazards of small plane crashes, but also the hazards and challenges of remote rescues.

On January 5, 1943, Harold Gillam was piloting a Lockheed 10-B, a dual-engine, eight-passenger plane, for Morrison Knudsen, a mining and engineering company. He was headed north from Seattle to Alaska in the middle of one of the most bitter winters in recent memory. Gillam had five passengers onboard the flight: copilot Robert Gebo, who was also general superintendent for Morrison Knudsen projects in Alaska; Percy Cutting, an aircraft mechanic; Dewey Metzdorf, an Anchorage hotel proprietor; and Joseph Tippets and Susan Batzer, employees of the Civil Aeronautics Agency (the forerunner to the FAA). While the weather had cleared slightly, conditions were still dangerous, and on the way to the first stop in Annette, in the southeastern corner of Alaska, the left engine failed. The ice and moisture were so thick that the right engine could not sustain the craft. Gillam radioed a quick message to the Annette airport, spotted a clearing on a mountainside, cut the engine and glided in for a crashlanding. Trees sheered off the right wing, the fuselage buckled, and the plane pitched into a snowbank where it

GETTING INTO THE COUNTRY THE HARD WAY

On September 19, 2000, a small plane circled the freighter *Chios Dream* in the Gulf of Mexico before plummeting into the water. The empty freighter, on its way from Colombia to New Orleans to pick up a grain shipment, headed for the crash site, where nine survivors—three men, three women, and three children—scrambled out of the small craft. The freighter recovered them, along with the body of a man who was killed in the crash. The freighter then met up with a cruise ship that had a doctor who could treat the survivors.

U.S. officials soon determined that the survivors were Cubans attempting to flee their country for asylum in the United States, and took them to Key West, Florida, for medical treatment. When the Cuban government learned of the crash, it accused those onboard the flight of hijacking the plane and demanded that they be returned to Cuba for prosecution. Once on U.S. soil, the refugees petitioned the government to stay, using the statute that allows immigrants to come to the United States if they can prove they were being persecuted. A two-day FBI investigation determined the plane had not been hijacked, and the U.S. government permitted the refugees to stay and join with Miami-area relatives, ending the controversy.

was buried by snow and covered by a tree that toppled down onto it.

All six onboard survived the initial crash, but Gillam had suffered a savage blow to the head, Gebo and Metzdorf had broken bones, Batzer had her wrist nearly severed, and Cutting and Tippets came through mostly unharmed. On the first day after the crash, the survivors built a fire, hoping rescue craft would come to their aid. Gillam had been farther off course than he had supposed, however, and severe weather was hampering the rescue effort. Batzer died of blood loss the next day. On the sixth day, Gillam set off to find help, despite his injuries. When five days had passed with no word from Gillam, Cutting set out to find help, but returned after two days without any luck. Finally, he and Tippets went out together, heading in a different direction from Cutting's original path. They wandered down to the water's edge of a deep bay and managed to flag down a passing Coast Guard ship. From there, a rescue was organized in which Coast Guard vessels parked themselves in inlets near the mountain, and rescuers climbed to the two stranded survivors. Jim Gill, one of the Coast Guard rescuers, recalls how the two were brought down the mountain:

> Gebo and Metzdorf had been carefully bundled up and lashed to sledges. Thus they could be pulled along, lowered or held back as the terrain demanded. We all took turns at this while several others scouted ahead for holes in the snowdrifts. In several more hours we reached the shoreline where we were met by another rescue group, including medical personnel. From there it was out over the ice to the ship. The two survivors were in terrible condition but they were going to live.[16]

Tragically, Gillam's body was discovered near one of the river inlets. After spending a remarkable thirty-three days on

▼ The pilot of this Cessna recovered from the injuries he sustained after coming down near a small pond in rural Georgia in November 2001.

the mountain, the other four survived, although Gebo and Metzdorf had severe injuries.

Beyond Rescue

Across the world, communities are formulating rescue plans for today's planes. Meanwhile, engineers are working toward a day when airplanes will carry between seven hundred and one thousand passengers. Safety and rescue experts see the potential for huge disasters. But such disasters would be less common, and rescues would become less important, if mechanical and human failures could be eliminated. Still, eliminating failures is one of the industry's toughest challenges, and even new technology does not seem to have all the answers.

CHAPTER THREE

Causes of Airplane Crashes

When a plane goes down, the initial concern is to find survivors and save lives. But immediately thereafter the focus changes to assessing the cause. It is vital for investigators to find the reasons behind crashes so that similar disasters can be prevented. But the causes of airplane crashes today are rarely traced to just one problem, and they are not easy to determine amidst the chaos and wreckage of a downed airplane. Complex factors generally combine to bring down a plane. Bad weather, like thunderstorms or fog, can compound pilot error, while small mechanical problems can affect other aspects of a plane's ability to function. In many cases, planes have flaws that may not be discovered until after disaster strikes. Still, investigators have done remarkable work in making sense of perplexing crashes, and as a result many safety features are regularly added to planes.

Flying Coffins

Early airplanes were primitive by today's standards, and unsatisfactory materials, unsafe cockpits, and poorly conceived fuel systems contributed to many deaths. The first planes built by the Wright brothers had the pilots lying precariously in the middle of the fuselage with little protection. Pilots were shortly sitting, but the aircraft were devoid of navigational technology, to say nothing of basic features like windshields, running lights, and so forth. More than thirty of the two thousand pilots flying in Europe during 1910 were killed in crashes, including the world's first midair collision. In the

▲ Amelia Earhart, shown here in June 1928 just before her pioneering transatlantic flight, was attempting an around-the-world trip when she disappeared in the South Pacific.

same year in the United States, daredevil pilots Ralph Johnstone and Arch Hoxsey alternated setting world altitude records, ultimately reaching almost ten thousand feet, before both died in separate crashes within weeks of each other.

By World War I, planes had advanced significantly, but safety was an afterthought. A memo written by a British officer during the war cited airplane losses because of accidents as one of the greatest wastes of money and manpower in the war. World War I airplanes were rickety and prone to mechanical failures. The cockpits were almost impossible to escape from, and the plane's materials were highly flammable. Wartime casualties were often due not to enemy aircraft or antiaircraft, but to mechanical failures. Commercial postwar aviation was hardly any less lethal—one out of every six pilots that worked for the U.S. Post Office's airmail service during the 1920s died, including thirty-one out of the first forty.

Many famous pioneering fliers paid for technological shortcomings with their lives. When American aviatrix Amelia Earhart and navigator Fred Noonan took off from New Guinea in the South Pacific on July 2, 1937, on the most difficult leg of their attempted round-the-world flight, they were trying to hit tiny Howland Island more than twenty-five hundred miles away with primitive navigational and communication tools. It would take only the slightest error or miscalculation for them to miss the island, by which time their fuel would be running low. Exactly what happened to them remains unclear almost seventy years later, but they never reached Howland. Despite a massive search, their plane was never found.

From mistakes in the military and in civilian flying, engineers have learned great lessons over time. Tough but flexible metals now resist cracking and breaking much better than earlier materials. Wing designs and engines have improved significantly, and backup power systems and safety mechanisms frequently keep one or more engines running when others have failed. Fire exits complete with slides have been added to help people evacuate the plane more readily, and seats are now flotation devices in case a plane crashes in water. Materials on the inside of the aircraft are now fire

WHAT GETS AN AIRPLANE OFF THE GROUND?

Lifting a multiton aircraft into the air is accomplished by a combination of straightforward physics and complex machinery. The overall process involves the difficult balancing of four main external forces acting on a plane: thrust, drag, lift, and weight. Thrust is the force an airplane generates to go forward. Engines primarily provide thrust. Drag is the friction and resistance that works in opposition to thrust; it is created by the force of air striking the aircraft in much the same way as water slows a hand being pushed through it. Lift occurs because of the speed and pressure differences of the air moving over and under a wing, while weight is the gravitational pull of the plane toward the ground.

A plane has several major parts to manage these forces. The engines provide sufficient thrust to overcome drag and allow the plane to move forward. As greater thrust is provided, air moves over and under the wings, causing lift. Each wing has a flap that can be used to slow the plane down by lowering it and increasing drag. Each wing also has an aileron, a movable piece that helps the plane turn and keeps it flying level. The horizontal part of the tail wing has elevators that can be moved up or down to control the plane's altitude. Vertical tail wings have rudders, flaps that move side to side to change the plane's direction.

A pilot must have complete mastery of not only these parts but numerous other mechanical and electronic parts to take off, fly, and land safely.

retardant to suppress the rapid spread of fire and noxious fumes. Even with all these improvements, gained mostly through tragic experience, airplane crashes continue to happen, and people continue to die. Sadly, many of the same causes that once brought about deaths still persist today.

Why Airline Windows Are Round

Newly designed airplanes undergo extensive testing before they are released into commercial service, and engineers try to simulate the stresses a plane will undergo over thousands of flights and through many years. Still, design flaws manage to slip through the tests and only begin to reveal themselves when planes start to fall from the sky. Such flaws can be difficult to discern once crashes start happening, and they are frequently costly, though crucial, to fix.

Some of the earliest and most disastrous design-related tragedies occurred on the first commercial jet aircraft, the British-built Comet. The Comet was designed and developed following World War II by famous British aeronautical engineer Sir Geoffrey de Havilland, and it quickly became the pride of England. The release of the aircraft into commercial service in 1952 caught the commercial aviation world, particularly the United States, flat-footed. The Comet could travel close to five hundred miles per hour, almost twice as fast as the then-popular, prop-driven Lockheed Constellation, and at altitudes of almost forty thousand feet.

During the second year of its release, however, the Comet developed a reputation for having the worst safety record of any aircraft on the market. On March 3, 1953, a Comet crash upon takeoff in Karachi, Pakistan, killed all eleven onboard—the first commercial jet fatalities in history. Two months later, a Comet attempted to fly through a violent storm over Calcutta on its way to cruising altitude. It broke up in midflight, killing all forty-three onboard. Authorities suggested that the plane was overloaded in the tail, though the debris was scattered over such a wide area it was impossible to gather enough wreckage for a complete investigation.

In January and April 1954, two more Comets traveling from Rome to London broke apart in midflight, killing a total of fifty-six more passengers and crew. Amidst rumors of sabotage, British authorities finally grounded the plane for definitive testing and investigation by the Royal Aircraft Es-

▲ The square windows on this prototype de Havilland Comet, shown here during an August 1948 test flight over the English countryside, turned out to be a factor in structural weaknesses tied to later crashes.

tablishment. Engineers recovered almost 70 percent of one of the crashed planes and painstakingly rebuilt it. Each part of the plane was minutely examined, and sections of the fuselage were subjected to underwater pressure tests.

The pressure tests proved to be revealing. The fuselage gave way in various circumstances, and engineers soon learned that the metal around the square windows was failing. Originally, engineers had predicted that the metal would not fatigue, or wear out, for ten years, but they had not counted on the stresses that built up around the corners of the square windows. After just one thousand hours of flying, the metal around these windows was failing. Rounded windows were installed and other modifications were also performed to beef up the Comet's relatively thin fuselage walls. It was a number of years before the Comet could once again be certified as a commercial aircraft, and de Havilland lost its market edge to American companies such as Boeing and Douglas. The exhaustive and thorough Comet investigation became a landmark event in aviation safety history, serving as a model for future investigations that unfortunately would also focus on design deficiencies.

A Suspect Cargo Door

The wide-cabin, three-engine DC-10 was a highly successful new airliner when recently merged McDonnell Douglas started building them in the late 1960s. It also had a fatal design flaw that managed to persist until the infamous crash of

Flight 981 in France on March 3, 1974, which claimed 346 lives. The Turkish carrier THY was flying a fully loaded DC-10 from Paris to London. Two years earlier the rear cargo door had blown off a similar DC-10 over Windsor, Ontario. The sudden cabin depressurization buckled the cabin floor near the door and disabled crucial control lines. The American Airlines pilot skillfully landed the plane without loss of life. The accident investigation easily pinpointed the blame: The cargo door was a new, outward-opening design. Earlier, inward-opening "plug" doors, because cabin pressure helped to keep them shut were virtually fail-proof. With an outward-opening door, cabin pressure could easily exert enough force to cause a catastrophic failure if the door was not fully and properly latched.

After the American Airlines incident, government regulators and DC-10 manufacturer McDonnell Douglas agreed that airlines needed to make a number of modifications to their DC-10s' cargo doors to prevent future accidents. One of these modifications had not been made to the THY DC-10, and a

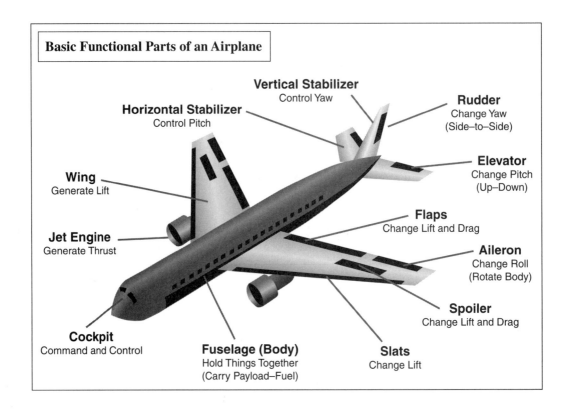

Basic Functional Parts of an Airplane

Vertical Stabilizer
Control Yaw

Rudder
Change Yaw
(Side–to–Side)

Horizontal Stabilizer
Control Pitch

Elevator
Change Pitch
(Up–Down)

Wing
Generate Lift

Flaps
Change Lift and Drag

Jet Engine
Generate Thrust

Aileron
Change Roll
(Rotate Body)

Spoiler
Change Lift and Drag

Cockpit
Command and Control

Fuselage (Body)
Hold Things Together
(Carry Payload–Fuel)

Slats
Change Lift

crucial warning card on the door, written in English, was unreadable to the Algerian-born baggage handler who shut the door. Barely ten minutes out of Paris's Orly Airport, at an altitude of eleven thousand feet, the cargo door blew open, depressurizing the cabin. Six passengers and some debris were sucked out, interfering with the second engine, which failed. Unlike the incident two years earlier, the pilots were unable to maintain control of the aircraft and it plunged into the ground while traveling at more than 500 miles per hour. No one survived.

The accident report once again faulted the cargo door design: "The underlying factor in the sequence of events leading to the accident was the incorrect engagement of the door latching mechanism before take-off."[17] In essence, the doors appeared to crew members to be locked, but were not. The huge loss of life finally galvanized regulators and engineers to mandate strict design changes that could more reliably prevent future DC-10 cargo door catastrophes.

To Err Is Human

While design flaws have led to tragic incidents, nothing is blamed so consistently and so often for crashes as pilot error. Since the 1950s, more than 50 percent of all accidents in which cause could be determined have been linked at least in part to pilot error. With so many elements to control and variables to assess, pilots can err in many ways. The largest category of pilot error is simply poor judgment—overshooting landing strips, failing to lift off properly, or misusing instruments. In many cases bad weather is a contributing factor. Fog or storms can limit visibility and reduce a pilot's margin for error. Finally, pilots can be sidetracked by mechanical issues. Faulty autopilots or data readouts can deceive pilots; fires in the cabin can cause confusion; malfunctioning parts can cause pilots to take actions they normally would not.

One of the most famous human error episodes highlighted not only pilot error but widespread institutional failure. In the late 1970s, the U.S. government began to deregulate the American airline industry, allowing airline companies more freedom in setting fares and establishing routes. One effect was to encourage the start-up of numerous small carriers such as Air Florida. It flew to cities up and down the East Coast, including Washington, D.C. Early in the

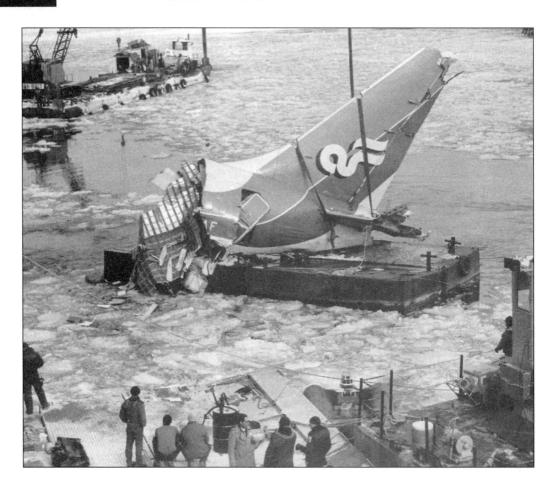

▲ The tail of Air Florida Flight 90 is plucked from the icy Potomac River and placed atop a recovery raft shortly after the tragic 1982 crash.

afternoon on January 13, 1982, a blizzard struck that city, closing schools and businesses and snarling traffic. Air Florida's Flight 90 with seventy-nine aboard was delayed because of the weather, but the captain nevertheless ordered the plane deiced and the aircraft readied for takeoff.

At last, one hour and fifteen minutes after its scheduled departure time, Flight 90 was cleared to back away from its gate. The snow was so heavy that one of the vehicles pushing the plane got stuck, and another with chains on its tires had to finish the job. On the way to the runway, the crew breezed through the preflight checklist, and Captain Lawrence Wheaton pulled close enough to other aircraft about to take off that he was able to melt the snow on the wings of the aircraft. But voice recordings and the subsequent investigation would reveal that the plane's *engine* deicing system was never activated. Shortly after takeoff, the plane's engines were unable to push the aircraft into a climb. The plane slammed into the city's Fourteenth Street Bridge, killing four motorists and crushing several cars before plunging into the icy Potomac River. Just five survivors were pulled from the frigid river.

The resulting investigation revealed more than just the failure of the pilot and his crew to deice the engine. The National Transportation Safety Board (NTSB), which investigates plane crashes, found that Wheaton and his copilot were young and inexperienced, that they had not been trained properly, that they had advanced too quickly into their positions, and that the company had mismanaged pilot training and procedures. Investigators also determined that Wheaton and his crew had made fatal mistakes in their operational procedures.

Ken Smart, an investigator for Great Britain's Air Accident Investigation Branch, praised his fellow investigators in the NTSB, saying,

> The investigation of the Potomac icing incident was probably the great watershed in this respect. It uncovered inexperience, unquestioned procedures, too rapid expansion, accelerated upgrading of pilots, and managerial blindness to risks, and the NTSB was quick to respond with the recruitment of several human behavior specialists.[18]

When the Military Makes a Mistake

A rare form of human error has resulted in some of the worst airplane disasters: military-related mistakes. Global tensions often put nations on high alert against spy planes and enemy attackers. On occasion, military commanders on the front lines make tragic decisions.

Such was the case on July 3, 1988, when the U.S. Navy cruiser *Vincennes* on patrol in the Persian Gulf mistook an Iranian airliner for an attacking jet. At the time, Iraq and Iran were fighting a war and U.S. warships were protecting oil tankers from attacks by Iran's ragtag navy. The billion-dollar *Vincennes* was one of the most advanced, and highly armed, warships in the world. Flight 655 out of Iran was loaded to near capacity with 290 people when it ventured out over the gulf. *Vincennes* officers in the ship's high-tech war room mistook the aircraft for an attacking plane similar to the Iraqi fighter that a year earlier had accidentally fired missiles at the USS

▶ The *Vincennes* cruiser, shown here at a South Korean port in March 2003, was one of the U.S. Navy's most advanced warships when it mistakenly shot down an Iranian jetliner in 1988.

Stark, killing thirty-seven U.S. sailors. The *Vincennes* radioed warnings to the plane to identify itself but the pilots were busy talking to air traffic controllers and never responded. When the unfortunate airliner came within ten miles of the *Vincennes*, the boat's skipper ordered a surface-to-air missile attack that blew the commercial aircraft out of the sky, killing all onboard. The Pentagon claimed "justifiable self-defense" but world opinion was less forgiving. A *Newsweek* investigation dubbed it a "naval fiasco" and blamed the "overeager captain" and "panicked crewmen."[19]

Israeli fighter jets also shot down a civilian Libyan Arab Airlines 727 on the afternoon of February 21, 1973, killing 108 people. The airliner had a compass problem that caused it to stray off course over Egypt's Sinai Desert, then occupied by Israeli military forces. When Israeli fighters approached the airliner, the French pilot apparently thought they were Egyptian jets. Whether warning shots were fired, or observed by the airliner crew, remains disputed. One crew member and four passengers managed to survive the cannon attack and subsequent crash.

Failure on Flight 011

In another noted case of human error, distraction among the crew and navigational incompetence led to tragedy. On November 27, 1983, Avianca Flight 011 was scheduled to fly from Paris to Bogotá with a stop in Madrid. On the approach to Madrid, the pilot and copilot of the 747 engaged in small talk and errors began to accrue. They missed one navigational checkpoint that helps to guide pilots in for landing. At a second point, the first officer entered into the plane's computer an altitude figure of 2,382 feet for a crossing marker instead of the correct figure of 3,282 feet. This innocent transposition of digits had the fatal effect of making the pilots think they were 900 feet higher than they actually were. As the plane descended perilously close to the ground, warnings from the computers began to sound. In particular, the ground proximity warning device began to go off. According to *The Indestructible Pilot*:

> Eventually, the Ground Proximity Warning system called: "Terrain, terrain. Whoop, whoop. Pull up. Terrain!" The captain took no notice. Ten seconds later, just before impact, he said calmly, "OK, OK!" Five seconds later, again he said, "OK!", disconnected the autopilot and slightly reduced the rate of descent.[20]

BROUGHT DOWN BY AN AIR-TO-AIR MISSILE

The *Vincennes* incident was one of the most grievous such military attacks on commercial airliners, but it was not unique. On September 1, 1983, a Korean Air Lines 747 en route from Anchorage, Alaska, to Seoul, South Korea, strayed far off course and entered Soviet airspace. Soviet fighter jets intercepted the airliner. When the airliner seemed to ignore warning cannon fire and blinking lights, even though the plane was minutes from leaving Soviet airspace, one of the fighters fired two air-to-air missiles that downed the plane and killed all 269 people onboard. Like the *Vincennes* incident, this is among the ten worst in history in terms of airplane fatalities.

Traveling at a speed of 160 miles per hour, the 747 hit a hill at an altitude of 2,249 feet with its landing gear and fourth engine. It then hit a second hill, where the ground sheared off a wing, the plane flipped, broke into five pieces, and landed upside down. All but 11 of 192 onboard perished. Ultimately, the flight navigators and the pilot were blamed for failing to follow correct procedures and for not heeding the warnings of their instruments.

Instruments Versus Experience

Highly publicized blunders like those that led to the Fourteenth Street Bridge crash and the Madrid crash can make people forget that flying a modern airliner is a tremendously difficult and challenging job. The Hollywood movies that show inexperienced people taking over during an emergency and heroically landing the craft are more myth than reality. Pilots are often the first to admit that, given the complex tasks they face, they can and sometimes do make mistakes. Only rarely, however, are such mistakes fatal for all aboard. Moreover, many pilots and others in the aviation industry warn against the attempt to remove all pilot error by, for example, letting computerized autopilots take over the flying. In fact, some pilots argue that flying has already become too instrument dominated and that pilots' judgment and experience have become too secondary to machinery that cannot properly correct mistakes.

Various instrument- and autopilot-caused crashes support such charges. On December 20, 1995, American Airlines Flight 965 was headed into Cali, Colombia, from Miami. The flight had been uneventful, and the pilots requested permission to begin their approach. The tower asked Flight 965 if it could take the direct approach into the airport and use runway 19 instead of going by the Cali approach. The pilot of Flight 965 signaled his willingness and began the direct approach. He was passing over Tulua as he entered the approach information into the autopilot system. Tulua was the beginning of the approach, but by the time the information marking Tulua was entered, the flight was already passing it.

When the autopilot was engaged, it attempted to realign the flight with Tulua by turning the plane east. The plane traveled east for only about one minute, but the pilot was now confused by the redirection and was unaware that the plane had deviated off course in the middle of a perilous canyon. He radioed the tower and asked directions on making an approach over another city, but the tower misunderstood his intention and directed him to a landing strip. Moments later, the plane crashed into a mountain at nine thousand feet, killing 158 of the 162 onboard.

Safety critics have said that had the pilot not been relying solely on instruments but had studied the terrain and known the approach, he would have realized the danger he was in. Critics further suggest that too much of the operation of a plane has become automated, and when the machines fail or misguide a plane, a pilot is often left confused and unable to

▼ Two men look at a large piece of wreckage from the crash of American Airlines Flight 965, which veered off course en route from Miami to Cali, Colombia, and crashed into a Colombian mountainside on December 20, 1995.

discern what is truly happening. Others point out that automated devices have made planes much safer and have saved them from midair and ground collisions.

Air Traffic Control Problems

Before a plane takes off in the United States, air traffic controllers in the tower put a given plane's flight information (where the plane is headed, when, and by what direction, as well as weather information and other factors) into a computer. That information is used to track the plane from station to station on its flight. Controllers use ground radar to track airplanes at the airport, and they use a separate radar to track airplanes in the local skies. The plane's transponder sends encoded radio signals to radar stations, letting the stations know where the plane is and what it is doing. As the plane travels, the flight information and tracking of the plane passes from zone to zone until it reaches the control tower of the airport where the plane will land. Special "final approach spacing tool" software tells controllers where the plane is headed, how large it is, and when it is expected. It also suggests the proper landing strip. This software helps controllers keep planes evenly spaced and prevents runways from being overburdened. Any errors in this complex system can lead to death and disaster.

Tower control mistakes can be particularly costly when they put two planes on collision courses. Air traffic control has improved over the years, partly in response to air disasters such as the one that occurred in Split, Yugoslavia, during the mid-1970s. The airspace over Yugoslavia had become particularly crowded by then, since the country was an aerial crossroads for flights moving over Europe. Unbeknownst to many, there had already been several near collisions over Yugoslavia because of the heavy traffic and increased demands on flight controllers' attention. On September 10, 1976, the shift change hour had arrived, and the lead traffic controller was due to be relieved. But the person taking his place was late for work, and the tired controller grew impatient. He turned operations over to an assistant controller and went looking for his replacement.

The volume of traffic at that time was so high that even a lead traffic controller would have had trouble managing.

JUGGLING 5,000 PLANES AT A TIME

During peak hours in the United States, there are some five thousand planes in the air. Juggling all those flights safely is a complex and highly technical task for air traffic controllers. Air traffic controllers use specialized hardware and software to track planes and communicate with pilots. The FAA's Air Traffic Control System Command Center oversees all air traffic control for the United States. It separates the United States into twenty-one zones or centers, which are then broken into smaller sectors. There is an Air Route Traffic Control Center for each zone that manages travel in and out of the zone until planes get close to airports. When planes get near airports, they are guided by Terminal Radar Control, which directs planes to the appropriate airport in a fifty-mile diameter and prepares the plane for landing. Planes then are governed by air traffic control towers at individual airports, which dictate takeoffs, landings, and ground traffic.

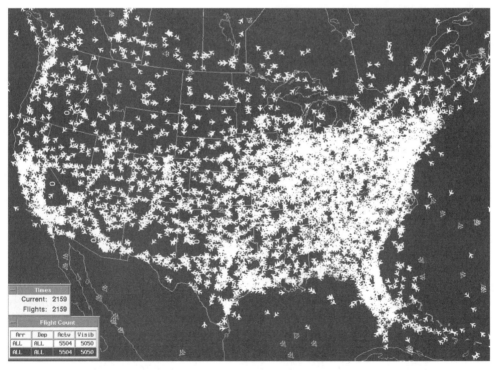

▲ Air traffic controllers sometimes juggle the flights of five thousand planes over the continental United States, as seen in this image from FAA's Air Traffic Control System Command Center.

Soon, the assistant was overwhelmed. When the superior finally brought the replacement in for the transition, the assistant was distracted by numerous messages coming in and by the converging plot points on the radar. Communication with the replacement only heightened the confusion, and the assistant ultimately cleared one aircraft for a climb that put it in the path of another. At the last moment, the assistant realized his mistake and ordered evasive moves, but it was too late. The wing of a British Airways Trident slashed through the cockpit of a Yugoslavian Inex Adria DC-9. Both planes crashed, killing all 176 onboard. The seven traffic controllers on duty that night were arrested, and the assistant was ultimately charged, tried, and sentenced to seven years in prison. In the end, he served only two years, and the rest of his sentence was dropped when the prosecutor made a powerful case that the assistant had not failed, the system had.

The Yugoslavia midair collision was a key moment in the history of air traffic control. The prosecutor pointed out the enormous stress on tired controllers and highlighted several procedures that were faulty and would naturally induce error. The aviation industry took notice and began to change air traffic control. Broader and more intensive training was introduced, and efforts were put in place to make sure controllers got sufficient rest.

Still, these measures have not prevented all tragedies. The infamous Canary Island and New Delhi crashes happened on takeoff. In both cases, better controller management could have saved the planes. Today, collision avoidance software has eased the problem somewhat, but there is continual pressure to allow more traffic in the sky. Air traffic control technology needs to be upgraded. Many U.S. traffic controllers are retiring, and few have been found to take their place. Critics believe midair disasters could increase as a result of these problems in the coming years.

Mechanical Mishaps

If obsolete equipment is problematic in air traffic control towers, faulty equipment in airplanes is deadly. Tragically, mechanical and maintenance failures have resulted in some of history's most tragic crashes. In fact, since 1950, approximately 20 percent of all crashes in which fault could be determined were caused by mechanical failure, and roughly 5 percent of all pilot error accidents were related to mechanical failures. Thus, mechanical failures are the second leading cause of airplane crashes.

One of the worst crashes related to mechanical failure occurred in 1979 when American Airlines Flight 191 lifted off from Chicago's O'Hare Airport. Investigators would later discover that the plane, a DC-10, had not only design flaws, but a history of poor maintenance. As the plane lifted off, a photographer waiting for another plane at O'Hare watched the plane and later said, "The left engine seemed to explode away from the wing although there was no smoke or flame." The witness watched the engine "come tumbling through the air, tumbling and tumbling, to the ground. There was still no flame."[21]

With an engine gone, the plane began a sharp roll to the left. The tower radioed the pilot, Walter Lux, asking if he wanted immediate clearance to land. Lux never answered. He was likely wrestling in futility with the now uncontrollable plane. A minute later, the plane, loaded with jet fuel, slammed into the ground and burst into enormous flames. A man standing outside his office building nearby said, "By the time I looked up, there was a rain of fire falling down on me."[22] Witnesses said the flames leapt to four hundred feet. The intense heat from the burning fuel kept many firefighters and rescuers from approaching the plane until the flames had burned down.

A local pastor arrived on the scene almost immediately. "It was too hot to really do anything but administer the last rites," he later related. "I said some prayers and gave a general absolution. I just walked around trying to touch a body here or there, but I could not. It was much too hot to touch anybody and I really could not tell if they were men or women."[23]

Debris was spread into a nearby trailer park. An old aircraft hangar, several cars, and a mobile home were destroyed. All 271 onboard were killed, as were two people on the ground. Aside from the September 11, 2001, terrorist attacks, the Flight 191 crash is the worst air disaster in U.S. history.

Multiple Failures

Investigation into this particular DC-10 crash revealed design, mechanical, and maintenance failures. Investigators ultimately concluded that the attachment points of the engine to the plane had design flaws and that they had not been properly maintained. Further, they found that the FAA had failed to oversee maintenance of DC-10s across the country, allowing dangerous practices to develop. Worse, manufacturers and airlines were not communicating sufficiently, and low-quality parts had gotten into DC-10 supply chains across the country. Finally, emergency warning systems that might have saved the plane failed, and procedures to handle such an incident had not been properly developed.

Investigators concluded that had the engine dropped off the plane at a higher altitude, the pilot could have used the other engines to fly safely to a nearby airport. No safety procedures had been developed, however, for incidents at such low altitudes. As a result of these findings, the FAA imposed strict new regulations and inspections for DC-10s, which led to better parts and greater adherence to sound procedures.

Sabotage and Terrorist Acts

While pilot errors, maintenance mistakes, and mechanical failures are prominent causes of accidents, it is the possibility of a terrorist act that strikes the greatest fear in many flyers. The first attempted plane hijacking occurred in 1931, and during the 1930s it was not unheard of for an angry person to sabotage a neighbor's crop duster. The threat posed by criminal acts directed at airplanes became much more significant as the airline industry developed. The first commercial plane bombing in North America occurred on September 9, 1949, when a bomb exploded in a baggage compartment of a Quebec Airways flight, killing twenty-three people. In 1955 a relative of a passenger put a bomb onboard a commercial flight out of Denver, killing forty-four people.

Such acts were relatively rare until the late 1960s, when attacks on commercial airlines took on a more political tone. Hijackers found that taking control of an airliner and holding passengers hostage brought media attention. Governments could be forced to negotiate issues relating to the release of political prisoners, for example. During the 1970s and 1980s there were scores of attempted hijackings and acts of sabotage on commercial aircraft worldwide. At least a dozen airline crashes during this time were due to sabotage or bombings.

Perhaps the most appalling of these terrorist acts occurred on December 21, 1988, over Lockerbie, Scotland. Pan Am Flight 103 had left London's Heathrow Airport bound for

New York when it disappeared twenty-five minutes into flight over Scotland. Bob Glaster, a retired policeman living in Lockerbie near the crash site, said, "The plane came down 400 yards from my house. There was a ball of fire 300 feet into the air, and debris was falling from the sky. When the smoke cleared a little, I could see bodies lying on the road. At least one dozen houses were destroyed."[24]

▲ In December 1988, the nose section of Pan Am Flight 103 came to rest in rural Scotland after a terrorist bomb exploded in mid-flight.

In addition to the 259 passengers and crew who were killed, 11 people on the ground in Lockerbie also died. Debris was widely scattered but investigators eventually found remnants of a bomb that had been placed in the cargo hold of the plane. More than a decade of investigation and international legal wrangling led to two Libyan suspects being tried in the Netherlands for planting the bomb. In 2001, one suspect was convicted and the other acquitted.

While tightened security since the early 1990s has greatly reduced hijackings, shootings, and airliner bombings, on September 11, 2001, nineteen Islamic extremists armed with box cutters managed to board two airliners in Boston, one in Newark, New Jersey and another in Washington, D.C. The resulting hijackings led to the deaths of some three thousand people, as the terrorists took over the cockpits and piloted the planes into New York's World Trade Center towers, the Pentagon, and (apparently thwarted by passengers) a field in Pennsylvania. The terrorist attacks of 9/11 prompted an overhauling of aviation security throughout the world. Cockpit doors are now reinforced and kept locked, a relatively simple precaution that would have prevented the 9/11 attacks. All passengers, crew, and luggage are also subjected to more extensive searches before being allowed onto aircraft.

Confounded by Complexity

Plane crashes are generally not caused by a single, easy-to-identify cause. Rather, multiple failures generally contribute to cause a disaster—a maintenance mistake may lead to a mechanical failure, or poor weather can contribute to a series of pilot errors. As a result plane crash investigations are fraught with difficulties. Modern commercial aircraft are exceedingly complex machines with millions of parts and sophisticated computerized equipment. A crash may burn and scatter debris, and wreckage in the ocean may not be recovered at all. Yet the effort is crucial to ensure safer flights in the future.

CHAPTER FOUR

Specialized Investigations

Within hours of a major airplane crash, media reports inevitably begin to speculate about what happened. The need to know what happened is understandable. After all, with more than 10 million flight departures every year in the United States alone, an undetected flaw in a common aircraft is reason for concern for millions of people. But full answers are usually not readily available. Investigating a crash is a grueling and often thankless task, and recovery experts are often faced with harsh weather conditions, mangled aircraft, and difficult terrain. The human aspect of a tragedy also cannot be ignored. Bodies, or body parts, often litter the ground. Personal articles, from a child's doll to a student's notebook, remind investigators of the halted lives of the victims. Back at the laboratory, researchers piece together plane parts, looking for clues about what happened.

The pressure to come up with quick answers is strong. The news media and surviving family members want immediate answers, and the aviation industry needs to know what adjustments to make as flights continue. But many investigations must face the challenge of conflicting witness reports and chaotic crash scenes, and the possibility of multiple causes. Coming up with firm answers can take months or even years.

How Reliable Are Witnesses?

In the aftermath of a plane crash, the news media and investigators on the ground inevitably seek out eyewitnesses. Those who have seen a crash may be able to provide investigators with clues about what might have gone wrong. But eyewitness testimony can be inconclusive at best and misleading at worst, as was evident from the problems associated with first-hand reports of the crash of TWA Flight 800 on July 17, 1996. The Boeing 747 took off from Kennedy International Airport in New York bound for Paris. Twelve minutes later and at a height of almost fourteen thousand feet over the Atlantic, an explosion rocked the plane and it disappeared from air traffic control radar screens. All 230 onboard died.

The investigation was a challenge from the start because the accident happened over water, making the search for debris particularly difficult. Worse, eyewitness reports were conflicting and confusing. People on a passing Saudi 747 reported seeing a green light streak past their plane. Two Air National Guard helicopter pilots reported seeing streaks of light heading for the TWA craft just before it exploded in a fireball. The pilots made statements to the FBI but did not claim to know what caused the streak of light. In addition, dozens of witnesses on the shore also reported seeing a streak of white light moving upward in the sky toward the plane just before it exploded.

These fast-spreading witness reports pointed to an obvious cause for the explosion that destroyed Flight 800: It was shot down by some type of missile. This possibility created a media sensation—were terrorists to blame? An even more disturbing scenario soon began to make the rounds on the Internet: Could an errant U.S. military missile have hit the aircraft?

An Exploding Fuel Tank

The eyewitness reports of a missile attack gathered steam when a French magazine published pictures purportedly showing radar images of objects streaking toward Flight 800 in its final moments. The initial tests of chemical residues on the plane's wing were also consistent with an explosion from a bomb or missile. The swirling rumors and missile claims led to the involvement of U.S. criminal investigation agencies such as the FBI. They immediately began to look into the theory that a U.S. Navy ship had mistakenly shot down the airliner in a missile training exercise.

In the end, the missile theories were effectively disproved. The navy was able to show that its ships had not been in the

HOW BLACK BOXES WORK

Older black boxes record information on magnetic tape, in much the same way cassette tapes record information. Thousands of these units are still in service, but they are no longer being built. Instead, airline manufacturers have turned to computerized units that record flight and voice information digitally. The information for the flight data recorder black box comes from a "flight data acquisition unit" at the front of the aircraft. It takes vital information from about one hundred separate sensors (in the case of magnetic tape recorders) or as many as seven hundred sensors (in the case of digital recorders) throughout the aircraft, which provide readings for everything from altitude to cabin pressure. Cockpit voice recorders pick up conversations from microphones and record noises in the cockpit. On magnetic tapes, they can store the last thirty minutes of sound on a flight. The tapes loop over and over, recording the newest sound and replacing the oldest sound. Digital recorders operate similarly, but can record two hours of sound.

▲ The cockpit voice recorder from an Alaska Airlines crash in the Pacific Ocean is held by the robotic arm of the remotely piloted undersea vehicle that retrieved it.

area and had not launched any missiles. The FBI performed a series of more thorough tests on the suspect chemical residues and firmly established that nothing other than jet fuel was involved. Investigators now believe that the light streaks may have been caused by flaming fuel bursting from the plane's engines just before the plane exploded.

The official investigation into Flight 800 took four years to recover plane debris from the sea, painstakingly reconstruct the disintegrated airliner, and test possible scenarios. Ultimately, investigators concluded that Flight 800's large center wing fuel tank, located beneath the fuselage between the two wings, had exploded. (This 747 also had three additional fuel tanks in each wing.) The root cause was ultimately traced to metal shavings left over from repairs. Small wires needed to keep fuel tank pumps operating were likely damaged by these shavings, allowing an electrical current to ignite the fuel-air mixture. The FAA ordered various corrective actions for airlines, including replacing sharp-edged fuel probes that could damage wires, keeping fuel pumps idle unless they were submerged in fuel, developing electronic devices that could suppress power surges in wiring, and installing protective sleeves on fuel tanks. From a historic perspective, these are only the latest in a long series of safety-mandated fuel tank reforms, since preventing fuel tanks from exploding on impact during crashes has been a problem vexing aviation since its earliest days.

Despite the thorough investigation, some questions remain. Conspiracy theorists and those who place great faith in the eyewitness reports continue to believe that a missile hit the plane and that the U.S. government has engaged in a cover-up.

Gearing Up the Investigation

The investigation into Flight 800 was the most extensive and costly of any U.S. plane crash study to that point in history. Numerous agencies participated, but the primary one was the National Transportation Safety Board (NTSB), whose four hundred employees investigate some two thousand aviation incidents annually as well as five hundred rail, marine, and other transportation accidents. The board has sophisticated tracking and communications systems, allowing its experts to

be among the first to learn of accidents and to begin gathering information even before officials arrive on the scene.

Much like investigative agencies in other countries, the NTSB is staffed with specialists skilled in accident investigations. The NTSB's crack team of lead investigators, called the "Go Team," handles the initial details. The agency, in explaining how it tackled the Flight 800 disaster, said:

> The purpose of the Safety Board Go Team is simple and effective: Begin the investigation of a major accident at the accident scene, as quickly as possible, assembling the broad spectrum of technical expertise that is needed to solve complex transportation safety problems. The team can number from three or four to more than a dozen specialists from the Board's headquarters staff in Washington, D.C., who are assigned on a rotational basis to respond as quickly as possible to the scene of the accident. . . . During their time on the "duty" rotation, members must be reachable 24 hours a day by telephone at the office or at home, or by pager. Most Go Team members do not have a

▲ A thorough crash site search is the first step in an accident investigation, such as seen here after the crash of a Luxair twin-engine plane in early November 2002.

suitcase pre-packed because there's no way of knowing whether the accident scene will be in Florida or Alaska; but they do have tools of their trade handy—carefully selected wrenches, screwdrivers and devices peculiar to their specialty. All carry flashlights, tape recorders, cameras, and lots of extra tape and film.[25]

Among the team's first orders of business for the Flight 800 crash were to specify that all air traffic control tapes be preserved, all cockpit recorder devices be found and preserved, and the manufacturer of the plane be contacted for safety and manufacturing data. With Flight 800, as with all other crashes, a portion of the team began assembling a history of the flight. They also began assembling biographies of the flight crew and details about their medical histories, information on the structure of the plane and the baggage it was carrying, transcripts of the conversations between the crew and air traffic control, radar data on the flight, and numerous other pieces of information.

Two of the team's most sought-after pieces of aircraft debris after a crash are the flight data recorder and the cockpit voice recorder, popularly known as black boxes. Finding them

▼ One of the engines recovered after the crash of TWA Flight 800 is unloaded from a barge at a Coast Guard station in Hampton Bays, New York, in August 1996.

can often reveal important clues, and in most cases these devices survive even the most traumatic collisions, explosions, and fires. That is because they are built tough: The newest units, which may cost up to $15,000, are contained within a cylinder made of aluminum on the inside, high-temperature insulation in the middle, and stainless steel on the outside. They are tested by being slammed into objects, scorched in 2,000° F heat, submerged in pressurized salt water, and battered in other ways.

The gathering of information begins even as the Go Team's initial response experts are heading to the area. The team typically flies by commercial or government planes, depending on circumstances and availability, but they arrive as quickly as possible. Once on the scene, investigation and recovery efforts begin.

Reassembling the Pieces of the Puzzle

Investigators say that there is no such thing as a typical crash site, but one challenge characterizes many: The aircraft is in an awful condition, and determining what part belonged where on the plane can be perplexing. Further, investigations may be complicated by difficult terrain or remote locations. For instance, investigators have pulled plane wreckage out of oceans and swamps, craters where the metal is essentially pulverized, and even a snake-infested mountainside in Ethiopia that could be accessed only by helicopter.

In the case of Flight 800, investigators grappled with the rolling seas of the Atlantic Ocean, about eight miles off the coast of Long Island. Some of the wreckage was floating on the surface while other pieces had sunk to the ocean floor. Vessels from the U.S. Navy, New York Police Department, and other agencies used high-tech sonar devices to find large pieces on the bottom of the ocean. (Sonar sends out sound waves through the water; when the waves hit objects, they bounce back, revealing the position of the objects.) In the first week, the recovery effort was aimed chiefly at finding bodies, and investigators found many in large portions of the fuselage and near wreckage of the wing. They also found the plane's black boxes within the first week. Crash investigators then began pulling up parts of the fuselage, the engines, and other sections of the plane.

Eventually, commercial shellfish trawlers were recruited to help. Their specialized equipment was able to salvage smaller pieces of the wreckage, including parts of the fuel tank where the explosion originated. The efforts of several agencies and the commercial trawlers led to the recovery of more than 95 percent of the plane, allowing investigators to piece it together in a hangar and gain vital clues about the crash.

Investigations are not always so successful. In crashes involving raging fires, clues are often incinerated. Rainy weather on mountainsides can wash away residues and other clues. And planes that disintegrate in the air over rough terrain can make it difficult to find vital pieces, including even the black boxes. Such obstacles can occasionally prevent investigators from finding the root cause for a crash, but such failures do not happen for lack of effort.

The Search for Clues

Small plane crashes that occur in remote locations often present difficult problems for investigators. Small planes typically do not have flight or data recorders, meaning that there may be little information about the sequence of events. Of course, the government also does not put the same investigative resources into the crash of a small plane, compared to what it does when a commercial airliner crashes.

Still, all crashes are investigated, and the public stakes are raised when a prominent person is among the victims. Such was the case of the airplane carrying Senator Paul Wellstone of Minnesota on October 25, 2002. Wellstone was with his wife, daughter, and five others on a chartered plane that crashed in a bog about two miles from the Eveleth-Virginia Municipal Airport in Minnesota. All onboard were killed, and the aircraft left behind fewer clues than in a typical commercial plane crash. There were no flight or data recorders, and the pilots indicated no problem before the plane plummeted into the trees.

Investigators performed all their usual checks, but have since worked particularly from the information at the scene. On arrival, they mapped the plane's four corners—the front, the tail, and the two wingtips—because how a plane crashes and the way it breaks up can reveal key pieces of information. For instance, in the Wellstone crash, the plane landed perpendicular to the runway, suggesting to investigators that the plane was well off course. The pilots apparently banked the plane sharply just before crashing, suggesting either confusion or some kind of mechanical problem. In addition, investigators have picked out as much wreckage as possible, calling their finds "Easter eggs" because even the smallest pieces of material can provide important information. Investigators say that a stretched filament the size of a human hair can indicate whether there was a fire onboard or not.

In the case of the Wellstone crash, the mystery has not been solved and the investigation continues. A preliminary report released by the NTSB in mid-December 2002 said that investigators were looking closely at the possibility of wing icing. The plane crashed in light snow and fog, and the

▼ Federal investigators comb through wreckage at the scene of a plane crash that killed Minnesota senator Paul Wellstone and seven others on October 25, 2002, in a remote area of northern Minnesota.

conditions might have made the plane unmanageable if the wings had indeed iced over. Investigators had found no problem with the engines and had ruled out some other types of mechanical failure. While the investigation continues, experts say that a final decision about the cause may be tough to make. One NTSB investigator has said of such cases, "To figure out one of these things, give me someone who is one-quarter engineer, one-quarter pilot, one-quarter psychologist—and one-quarter soothsayer."[26]

Into the Lab

After investigators have sufficiently studied the actual crash site, they take the airplane parts back to the laboratory for in-

▼ After debris from TWA Flight 800 was recovered from the Atlantic, investigators painstakingly reconstructed the demolished jetliner to find out what went wrong.

vestigation. As this happens, metallurgists, engineers, meteo-rologists, and other experts combine their efforts in intensive investigations. Using sophisticated technology, they build models of planes and create elaborate computerized anima-tions to simulate different crash theories. They test specific airplane parts to find weaknesses. They also study weather re-ports, maintenance records, and information on pilots' phys-ical and mental health. The work is painstaking, and the clues do not always add up to easy solutions.

In the case of Concorde Flight 4590, which crashed on takeoff outside of Paris in July 2000 after hitting a piece of metal on the runway, the investigative techniques helped firmly establish how the tire burst led to the fuel tank explo-sion. When asked about reconstructing the crash of the Con-corde, David Learmount of *Flight International* magazine explained, "With the debris metallurgists can distinguish between parts which were damaged in the tire burst and airborne fire and those which were damaged by the crash and subsequent fire. The main scientific and engineering exper-tise applied is metallurgy and forensic chemistry, as well as previous experience in the field."[27]

But in the case of TWA Flight 800, things were not so clear. Investigators knew the explosion had happened in the center wing fuel tank, but a definitive answer for what ignited the fuel remains elusive. The salvage crew never found one of the missing fuel pumps for the center tank, nor many of the small wires that might have provided revealing clues. The destruc-tive forces unleashed during an airplane explosion or colli-sion are sometimes enough to hinder even the most thorough investigation.

CSI: Lockerbie

Suspicions that TWA Flight 800 was the work of saboteurs or terrorists prompted a criminal investigation. Although in the end no evidence of an attack was found, a different outcome followed the meticulous criminal investigation after Flight 103 exploded over Lockerbie, making it a classic case in air-plane forensics.

Flight 103 was twenty-five minutes late taking off. Had it been punctual, the time bomb the airliner carried would have exploded over the ocean, and the sea could have swallowed up

THE CHALLENGE OF 9/11

The worst plane disasters in history are the September 11, 2001, terrorist attacks that brought down the two World Trade Center towers in New York City. Approximately twenty-eight hundred people died, and the collapsing towers created a nightmarish rescue, recovery, and investigation scene. With so many people involved from so many agencies, sorting out the mess was a monumental effort.

Once the towers came down, the New York Fire Department and other rescue workers immediately began looking for survivors. Along with numerous volunteers they formed the well-known "bucket brigades" that soon faced a problem: Officials from the FBI and the NTSB did not want criminal evidence from the destroyed airliners tampered with. Arguments ensued over what could be moved

where. As federal investigators pieced together background checks on the passenger list, cell phone records from the doomed planes, and air traffic control communications, they quickly linked the disaster to fundamentalist Islamic terrorists. The focus of the investigation shifted from the World Trade Center site to the lives of the terrorists, the places they had visited, and the security measures that had failed.

Meanwhile, with the FBI and NTSB gradually withdrawing from the scene, New York City and the regional Port Authority took over the rubble removal and recovery efforts. They oversaw the police and fire agencies who continued to search for bodies even while the agencies rolled in heavy machinery to the site, since the rubble was simply too massive for human handling.

nearly all important clues of terrorist involvement. Tragically for residents of Lockerbie, but fortunately for investigators, the explosion over land would eventually yield the clues to the killers. As Gary Katz, a Canadian Broadcast Company news correspondent writes, "You might say that the 11 victims in the village of Lockerbie gave their lives that the perpetrators might be caught."[28]

It took investigators merely a week to discover that the plane had been brought down by a bomb. Despite the debris being spread over a large area, investigators pieced together everything, particularly parts of suitcases that appeared to have come from the site of the blast. Most importantly, forensics experts focused on two containers, a metal case and a fiberglass case, that had been put on the plane in Frankfurt, Germany. When as many pieces as possible were assembled, experts concluded that the blast had originated inside the metal container and had done immediate damage to the fiberglass container. As this experiment was going on, forensics experts at the Royal Armaments Research and Development Establishment discovered a telltale piece of a radio cassette player in the metal case. Experts concluded that the cassette player had been fitted with a bomb.

Using this information, investigators traced the bag's origins and gradually built a case over the years that pointed at two Libyan nationals. The hunt included testimony from a Libyan defector to the United States who turned over information against the two. Negotiations between the Libyan government and the British government finally led to the two

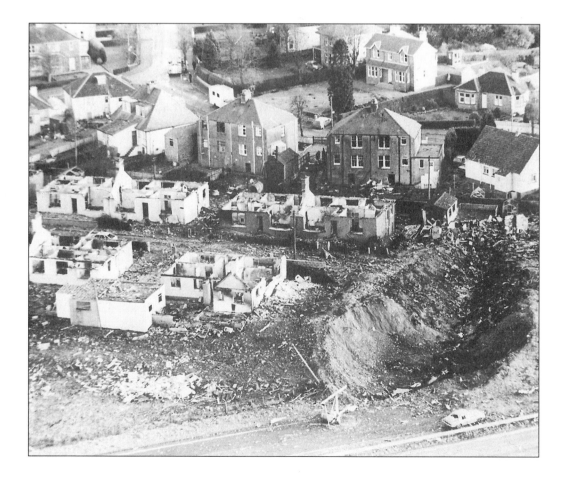

▼ Wrecked houses and a deep gash in the ground are evidence of the devastation caused by the crash of Pan Am Flight 103 into the Scottish village of Lockerbie.

men's extradition to Great Britain, where the trial began in early May 2000 and ended in January 2001. One of the men, Abdelbaset al-Megrahi, was convicted. Megrahi's 2002 appeal was denied, and he sits in a Scottish prison, still maintaining his innocence. Family members of those who died in the disaster continue to press authorities to find out who else might have helped Megrahi in the attack.

The Best Guess Possible

In the case of the Lockerbie disaster, uncertainty about all culprits involved remains. In accidental cases like the Paul Wellstone crash, the true cause may never be fully established, despite the best intentions and methods of an investigative crew. Still, the investigation is critical to finding and addressing flaws in pilot performance and airplane structure. But even with sophisticated technology and teams of experts, the causes of many crashes remain elusive. Experts sometimes grimly joke that when they die they hope to talk to the pilots of fallen planes to see how accurate their investigation results really were. In many cases, there is no way to know. But the search is made worthwhile by the advances it yields and the safety brought to thousands of others in the skies.

CHAPTER FIVE

Safety Steps for the Future

Thorough crash investigations around the world have led to design and mechanical improvements throughout the history of aviation. The last two decades, in particular, have seen remarkable developments in airplane safety features and procedures. This is because investigations have become more adept at diagnosing problems, while at the same time aviation technology has improved. Even so, annual accident rates have remained virtually unchanged since 1980. Perhaps more disturbing, while accident rates have remained unchanged, the number of flights has grown vastly over the last two decades, meaning that more and more people are involved in airplane crashes.

No doubt many features have saved lives, but there is plenty left to do. And though certain problems are easily diagnosed, changing behaviors and policies in the highly competitive airline industry is a particular challenge. Government regulators, air traffic controllers, and safety inspectors often find themselves in conflict with airline officials, pilots, and others as they try to balance safety concerns with cost, convenience, scheduling, and other factors. "There is, of course, an enormous incentive to make commercial aviation safe," notes Charles Perrow, author of *Normal Accidents: Living with High-Risk Technologies*. "Airline travel drops after large accidents; airframe companies suffer if one of their models appears to have more than its share of accidents."[29] Engineers, politicians, and industry officials are all wrestling with the best ways to reduce and eliminate plane crashes and improve survival rates in accidents.

Wanted: Alert and Rested Pilots

On April 3, 1996, a U.S. Air Force plane carrying U.S. commerce secretary Ron Brown and thirty-four others approached Dubrovnik airport in Croatia. Although storms covered the area, the crew proceeded on its approach. Just short of the airport, the plane slammed into a mountain, killing all onboard. A U.S. Air Force investigation primarily blamed the pilots for failing to follow proper navigational procedures on landing. Investigators also said that the airport was poorly designed, the navigational equipment at the airport and on the plane was inadequate for an instrument-guided approach, and the airport rules relating to the maximum altitude on the approach were flawed. While the pilots were criticized in part for their willingness to land at an airport the air force had already deemed dangerous and inappropriate for U.S. aircraft, other investigators have found that many of the pilots' procedural errors may be attributed to a factor that has become all too common: pilot fatigue.

Pilot fatigue has been blamed for causing pilots to misread signals about the aircraft, misunderstand proper navigational techniques in crucial situations, and fail to react to dangers. According to a report on the air force crash prepared for the FAA:

> Although the pilots detected an error on approach a full minute before the crash, they made no attempt to correct the error—a common characteristic of fatigue. This is due to a reduced level of adherence to one's normal standard and a reduced ability to cognitively make a connection between cause and effect. One may recognize a problem but not translate its effect due to lack of full comprehension of the situation or simple failure to initiate an action.[30]

Pilot fatigue standards have become a hotly debated issue in the United States. Airlines can currently keep pilots on duty for a maximum of sixteen hours in any twenty-four-hour period, and they can keep pilots flying for a maximum of eight hours during that duty time. No guidelines govern when a pilot can get the best type of rest for the body, however, and critics argue that today's standards cause pilots to miss sleep even when they are off duty.

Near Disaster at Salt Lake City

A notable example of fatigue contributing to a near disaster occurred on a landing at Salt Lake City Airport on January 22, 1989. The pilot of a 707 out of Honolulu started to fly visually rather than by his gauges at an altitude of three hundred feet, expecting to exit the low cloud cover and see the runway. The poor visibility extended lower than he expected, however, and he did not spot the runway off to his left until his altitude was just two hundred feet above the ground. At this point he lost his depth perception, he later admitted. Even so, rather than abort the approach he decided to try to use the altitude he had to align the plane with the runway. During the attempted maneuver he dragged his left outboard engine on the runway, creating a sixty-foot-long, one-inch-deep gouge on the runway. He nevertheless managed to land the plane without injuring any of his no doubt startled passengers.

▼ A number of factors caused the April 1996 plane crash that claimed the life of U.S. commerce secretary Ron Brown.

NTSB investigators later determined that the pilot had been on duty for more than eighteen of the thirty previous hours and that he had flown for almost fourteen of those hours. While he had had more than eleven hours off between duty periods, his circadian rhythm—his pattern of sleep and wakefulness—had been so thoroughly disrupted that he had been able to sleep only one hour. In its final report, the NTSB cited pilot fatigue as a major cause of the near disaster.

Airline pilots currently are pushing for changes in the FAA regulations. While airline companies and some FAA officials have pushed to extend the eight-hour flying time rule, pilot unions remain adamantly opposed, saying that pilots are less vigilant beyond eight hours. But the airline pilots face opposition. The Air Transport Association, a group representing major airlines, says that reductions in pilot duty times increase plane delays and aggravate passengers.

The Battle over Air Traffic Control

Disagreements about improving safety and meeting safety challenges extend well beyond the debate over pilot fatigue. The air traffic control system is currently in transition, and many industry watchers are nervous. A gloomy 1997 report commissioned by the U.S. government and published by the National Civil Aviation Review Commission said that airplane congestion in the skies was growing worse and that if the industry failed to improve, a major airline disaster could occur every seven to ten days in 2010. The commission found that air traffic control was overburdened, that many centers had not had significant technological upgrades in more than thirty years, and that few airports had been recently built or expanded, meaning the increasing number of planes would have limited sky space for takeoffs and landings.

The gloomy predictions seemed to be borne out as the years progressed since 1997. Flight delays increased a whopping 90 percent between May 1997 and May 2000, despite FAA rule changes designed to improve air traffic control efficiency. In 2000, the FAA released rules that shortened the time between takeoffs of aircrafts, believing that this would reduce delays. But the measures drew fire from safety groups, who said the move dangerously reduced the margin of error. Worse, legislation designed to encourage aviation competition and the growth of upstart airlines pushed more flights into the air, increasing the load on air traffic controllers. Delays rose 55 percent from October 1999 to October 2000, as air traffic controllers struggled to keep pace with all the extra traffic in the sky. The offshoot of the extra traffic, safety critics warn, is that disasters will begin to occur more often.

The U.S. air traffic control industry is also facing a personnel shortage in the coming years, and inexperienced traffic controllers could lead to increased accidents or delays or both. The shortage dates back to 1981, when President Ronald Reagan fired more than eleven thousand striking air

traffic controllers and ordered new controllers put on the job. An entire new crop of controllers came into the profession, and 70 percent of today's twenty thousand controllers will be eligible to retire by 2011. (Current FAA rules say a controller can retire after twenty-five years of service or when he or she reaches age fifty. Controllers hired as replacements in the 1980s must retire at age fifty-six.) FAA recruiters say they are aggressively pursuing new talent and foresee no shortage of workers in the near future, but air traffic safety experts disagree. They say the FAA has a policy of replacing a controller only when he or she leaves the profession, and thus they fail to account for the long training time, three to five years, involved in creating a fully functional controller. President John Carr of the National Air Traffic Association says the FAA policy could hurt air traffic control severely if it is not changed: "We've always said controllers are like runways—it takes three to five years to make a good one. We need to hire a bubble of controllers that will

▲ The federal government is constantly investing in modern equipment and training new personnel to keep the nation's complex air traffic control system running.

move our National Airspace System smoothly through the next decade without the turbulence of short staffing and its numerous associated problems."[31]

The air traffic control system faces many challenges, but officials are scrambling to meet the needs and ensure safe flights. The FAA is pressing ahead with plans to update air traffic technology. Officials are installing satellite global-positioning systems in towers across the country. This new technology makes it easier for controllers to track planes and gives controllers an effective tool for preventing collisions. Further, the FAA has streamlined procedures among towers and with airlines to improve the management of air traffic throughout the country and the world. Finally, the FAA is beginning to address concerns about its aging work force. It is recruiting younger controllers and studying other measures to bring qualified people onboard.

Improving Safety Features on Planes

The past two decades have seen numerous safety innovations that have increased both air traffic controllers' and pilots' efforts to prevent a crash. Sophisticated cockpit technology has helped take much of the guesswork out of pilots' hands. Pilots are better able to perform takeoffs and approaches because airliners are now equipped with collision-avoidance technology, and electronic landing beacons help line planes up to runways while keeping airports from being overburdened.

Safety efforts have also successfully focused on passengers' ability to survive a crash. As the NTSB notes:

> There are two ways to prevent fatalities in air travel: by preventing accidents, and by protecting aircraft occupants in the accidents that do occur. A reduction in accident rates provides an indication of the success of accident prevention; examining occupant survivability can indicate the positive results from occupant protection. The importance of examining occupant survivability in aviation accidents is twofold: (1) it can help to dispel a public perception that most air carrier accidents are not survivable, and (2) it can identify things that can be done to increase survivability in the accidents that do occur.[32]

Airlines are looking at ways, for example, to make seats with better restraints or an increased ability to absorb

CAN PASSENGERS INCREASE THEIR SURVIVAL ODDS?

One of the greatest dangers to passengers is a false belief about airplane safety. As U.S. airline travelers know, each flight in the United States begins with a safety demonstration. All too often, people ignore these demonstrations because they feel that if a plane crashes, there is little they can do to survive anyway. Some passengers believe that certain parts of the plane are safer than others. Experience has proven this idea false, although in an emergency evacuation passengers closest to doors have the best chance of escaping. Studies suggest that the most important steps passengers can take are to listen to the safety presentation and familiarize themselves with the location of the safety exits.

Understanding survivability may help passengers perk up a bit during demonstrations. While it is true that collisions with terrain or midair explosions are particularly lethal, most crashes occur on takeoff or landing, and many of those involve fires or fumes that are survivable if passengers act appropriately. The guidelines given in safety instructions are designed to get all passengers off a plane within ninety seconds if they cooperate and do as instructed. Tragically, many crashes have involved fires that did not become lethal for more than two minutes but still managed to take lives.

the energy of an impact. The FAA has recently issued regulations requiring that all new commercial aircraft use seats that have been specifically designed and tested for aviation use.

Airplane disaster investigations have shown that smoke and fumes cause more deaths than the flames themselves, so airlines have installed seat cushions, insulation, and other materials that are fire and smoke resistant. Within recent years aviation standards in the United States have been upgraded to require that airliners install floor lighting (since overhead lights may be obscured by smoke during an emergency); provide smoke detectors and fire extinguishers; and install cargo compartment liners to protect passenger cabins from cargo fires.

Reducing Fuel Tank Explosions

Reducing the risk of fire is also being addressed at the design stage, since fuel system spills and explosions are particularly

In December 1984, the FAA crashed a remote-controlled Boeing 720 to test a fuel additive that, unfortunately, failed to prevent a fiery explosion from demolishing the plane.

disastrous. Center wing fuel tanks, the culprit in the TWA Flight 800 explosion, remain a concern. At least two additional center wing fuel tank fatal explosions suggest that mostly empty tanks near warmed up engines can reach explosive temperatures. In 1990 a Boeing 737 that had been sitting for hours on a hot runway in Manila, the Philippines, experienced a center wing tank explosion, killing eight people. Most recently, on March 3, 2001, a Thai Airways plane exploded on a hot runway in Bangkok. The plane had been on the runway running its air conditioners for forty minutes. Air temperatures were above 90° F, and the tank was low when it exploded, killing a flight attendant and wounding seven others. Investigators have found that the combination of a hot day, overheated air conditioners, and a low fuel tank can be explosive. According to *Air Safety Week* editor David Evans:

The Thai Airways accident brings to 17 the number of fuel tank explosions that have occurred on jet airliners since the first event on a B707 in 1959. All told, about 550 people have been killed. Although the reigning philosophy has been to accept the presence of flammable vapors and to vigorously hunt down and eliminate all potential ignition sources, the toll exacted thus far is stark proof that the current design philosophy is a failure.[33]

After the Flight 800 disaster, the NTSB recommended that the FAA impose new safety regulations on the airlines that would make the fuel-air mixture less volatile. Pumping inert nitrogen into fuel tanks, for instance, would displace air and make the tank atmosphere safer from explosion. The military has used this technique for years, though it has never made it into the commercial realm. But five years after the NTSB recommendation, little had changed. The inaction was a source of frustration to some NTSB officials, who note that their agency investigates crashes and offers recommendations but that the FAA enforces aviation regulations. The NTSB's Director of Air Safety, John Clark, in an interview given in 2001, said after the Thai Airways disaster:

> The response to the center wing tank explosions and some of the actions that we'd like to see taken to prevent them aren't coming about, and that's a big concern. In fact, the center wing tank is on our most wanted list for improvements, so both the center wing tank issue and the fuel-air explosion issue are very active in our minds and we're very actively involved in them. It does give us concern that some of these are being handled by FAA [Aviation Rulemaking Advisory] Committees that routinely take a lot of time. The FAA should move faster on these issues.[34]

The FAA, in its defense, must study all recommendations closely and weigh them against industry demands and other factors. The FAA notes that it has been working with a division of the National Aeronautics and Space Administration (NASA) on the issue and has recently awarded four contracts to engineering firms to develop safer fuel tanks. The companies will explore ways to pump inert gas into the tanks and will look at other possible solutions to the problem as well.

The Cost of Safety

Part of the reason the FAA may take considerable time to alter safety regulations is that it must balance competing demands from different parts of the aviation industry. This was evident in the pilot fatigue issue, with pilot unions at odds with airline management, and in the center wing fuel tank issue, with pilot and consumer groups calling for reforms while the airlines called for further study. In these and other safety issues, the economic factor often plays a major role. With the high cost of fuel, the expenses of a skilled labor force, and the investment

▶ On June 27, 1996, during a news conference held in a Miami hangar, NTSB official Robert Francis points to pieces from the crash of ValuJet Flight 592.

needed to build or retrofit planes, airlines face continual challenges in making profits and growing their businesses. Further, the competition is keen, and start-up airlines face huge costs in launching their businesses.

The economics of the U.S. airline industry took a turn for the worse after the September 11, 2001, terrorist attacks caused consumers to reduce their flying. But the attack only worsened a situation that was already in progress. When profits shrink, airlines look to cut costs, and safety may be a casualty. This can be seen in a number of ways, from fewer mechanics and reduced inspection schedules to subcontracting maintenance and adding dangerous cargo to passenger flights. These were among the factors that resulted in the infamous crash of a ValuJet DC-9 in Florida's Everglades on May 11, 1996.

ValuJet Flight 592 lifted off from Miami International Airport and headed north for its destination of Atlanta, the start-up airline's corporate home. Just six minutes later, the pilots reported that they were losing all their systems. Cries of "Fire!" could be heard in the cabin. The pilots turned around and received permission to make an emergency landing. Minutes later, the jet plunged into the Florida Everglades twelve miles north of the airport, and all 110 onboard died.

The investigation of the ValuJet accident revealed a start-up airline struggling to cover costs and turn a profit, in this case at the expense of safety. In an extensive review of the crash, and the airline as a whole, William Langwiesche of the *Atlantic Monthly* commented on the cut-rate approach of the airline, saying:

> Pilots were not the only low-paid employees at ValuJet—flight attendants, ramp agents, and mechanics made a lot less there than they would have at a more traditional airline. So much work was farmed out to temporary employees and independent contractors that ValuJet was sometimes called a "virtual airline." . . . ValuJet was helping the entire industry to understand just how far cost-cutting could be pushed. Its flights were cheap and full, and its stock was strong on Wall Street.[35]

Exploding Oxygen Canisters

Langwiesche and others cite numerous maintenance and safety failures that occurred across the organization and in the FAA. The investigation revealed that the root cause of the

ValuJet 592 crash was outdated oxygen canisters that ignited in the cargo hold, creating a fierce fire that destroyed flight control systems. The oxygen canisters, which provide emergency oxygen to the mouthpieces that drop over passenger seats during an emergency, had been removed from an airliner that ValuJet was having refurbished by a subcontractor. ValuJet gave the subcontractor specific safety instructions for the packing and transfer of the canisters, but the subcontractor did not follow them. No ValuJet overseer checked to see if procedures had been violated. It turned out that the canisters were missing vital safety caps and had not been fired off. (The canisters use a tiny explosive charge to release their oxygen; firing them off would have emptied them of their flammable contents.) The canisters sat for a time in a hangar storage area. When the space was needed for something else, a shipping clerk who was not totally familiar with the canisters' contents packed them improperly and mislabeled them as empty. They were later loaded on the ill-fated plane. Lacking the safety caps, routine jiggling caused one or more to trigger and catch the cargo hold on fire.

The FAA cited ValuJet for not following appropriate safety and maintenance procedures. The agency also came under criticism for not taking a more active role—it had assigned just three inspectors to ValuJet. The FAA had also received prior reports about exploding oxygen canisters but had not bothered to try to prevent them from being shipped as cargo aboard passenger airlines. The Department of Transportation did impose an emergency ban on the shipment of oxygen canisters after the crash.

The series of mishaps that resulted in the ValuJet 592 tragedy was nearly fatal for the airline as a whole. It was grounded for several months. It returned later in 1996, and it continued to fly, but eventually changed its name to AirTran.

Protection Against Terrorism

While regulators have worked in the last several years to balance safety concerns with airlines' needs to make profits, security is another major issue in the industry. The 9/11 attacks highlighted the holes in U.S. airport security. Terrorists made it past security with box cutters that they later used to commandeer the planes. Further, many of the terrorists had got-

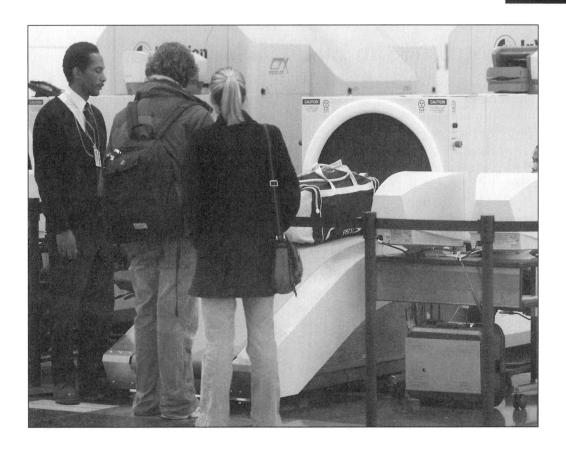

ten into the country without visas, and some were even under some federal suspicion before the attacks.

▲ In January 2003, baggage screeners at a Washington, D.C. area airport use a new explosives detection system to check passengers' luggage.

The first major action taken after the attacks was a revamping of airport security services. In the past, security services were contracted out by airlines to security companies. But a law passed by Congress in late 2001 required that security screeners be federal employees. Through 2002, the government aggressively recruited security screeners and trained them to take over airport security. On November 19, 2002, airport security came under federal control, directed by the Transportation Security Administration. The new security officers check carry-on baggage more rigorously and perform far more random searches of passengers.

In addition to these measures, the federal government mandated baggage screening machines that would examine checked luggage for bombs and weapons. Airports were to have these machines in place by December 31, 2002. Not all

INSECURITY AND SMALL PLANES

In October 2001 Canadian journalist Jacquie Perrin flew her small plane near Toronto's landmark CN Tower and over the Pickering Nuclear Power Plant in order to show how easy it would be to fly into such targets. The pilot also noted that because she belongs to a flying club, she must show identification, medical record, and log book before taking a plane out, but clubs and small airports generally ignore what she takes on a plane. Security experts say that many small airports do not bother with identification or baggage checks, and that the new security measures at major airports may prompt terrorists to consider using a small plane. Small plane trade groups have countered that small planes generally lack the fuel, and the cargo capacity, to be an explosive threat any greater than the tens of millions of cars and trucks driving around the country. In separate small plane incidents shortly after September 11, 2001, a suicidal teen flew a stolen Cessna into the side of a Tampa, Florida, building, killing only himself, and a small plane crashed into a skyscraper in Milan, Italy, killing the pilot and two others.

airports were able to comply, but all have backup measures in place, like bomb-sniffing dogs, until they can comply.

While security has increased dramatically at commercial airports in North America since 9/11, most safety experts agree that less has been done about security at the thousands of community airports that serve small private planes. Some security experts worry that unless things change, it will only be a matter of time before a terrorist uses a small plane as a public weapon. In early May 2003, an advisory that the U.S. Department of Homeland Security sent to the Aircraft Owners and Pilots Association warned that the Islamic fundamentalist terrorist group al-Qaeda has long considered attacking American targets using small planes or charter aircraft. Federal officials noted:

> Recent reliable reporting indicates that al-Qaeda was in the late stages of planning an aerial suicide attack against the US Consulate in Karachi. Operatives were planning to pack a small fixed-wing aircraft or helicopter with explosives and crash it into the consulate. This plot and a similar plot last year to fly a small explosive-laden aircraft into a US warship in the Persian Gulf demonstrate al-Qaeda's continued fixation with using explosive-laden small air-

craft in attacks. General aviation aircraft that were loaded with explosives to enhance their destructive potential would make them the equivalent of a medium-sized truck bomb.[36]

The Latest Threat: Shoulder-Fired Missiles

On November 28, 2002, al-Qaeda terrorists demonstrated that they could also pose a grave danger to airliners by firing shoulder-launched missiles at an Israeli charter flight lifting off in Kenya. The missiles failed, though they came

◀ The tail of a small Cessna hangs from a Tampa building after an apparently suicidal fifteen-year-old crashed the plane on January 5, 2002.

dangerously close—the pilots reported seeing the missiles' smoke trails near the aircraft. The missiles almost certainly missed their target because they were not the most advanced weaponry, like the sophisticated U.S.-built Stinger missiles that seek out engine heat. Stinger missiles and other heat-seeking varieties, however, have gained worldwide circulation and could be obtained by terrorists. Even less-accurate missiles like the ones fired in Kenya could do serious damage if used within close range. The Kenya attack thus posed troubling new questions about airline safety.

While military aircraft possess devices meant to throw off heat-seeking and other types of missiles, commercial airliners do not, and they are big, slow-moving targets. Takeoffs and landings are particularly perilous because commercial carriers are close to the ground and not able to maneuver rapidly without endangering passengers' lives. Security experts are now considering ways to protect commercial airliners against missile attacks. Some have argued that airlines should equip their planes with decoys and other missile-diversion technology. But such systems are expensive and do not provide guarantees of success. While no major airlines or countries have moved to such measures yet, many fear the day when a terrorist missile finds its target.

A Troubled Future for Aviation

Behind the scenes, U.S. officials are taking matters a step further. Software that profiles passengers, for example, might alert airlines to criminals with terrorist ties. Critics say such software is intrusive, could single out innocent people, and is unlikely to actually work. Even with heightened passenger security, airplane tarmacs are open and difficult to police. Experts worry, for example, that terrorists could plant a bomb on a plane if they had access to the loading carts used after luggage screening.

While dangers persist not only due to the threat of terrorism but also from mechanical failures, human error, and design flaws, flying remains an exceptionally safe form of travel. Today's aeronautic engineers are focused on making the skies both safer and more accessible to greater numbers of people. Advances in aviation will soon allow much larger planes capable of carrying as many as one thousand passengers. In fact a modified 747 airlifted almost eleven hundred refugees from Ethiopia in 1991. Preventing crashes and terrorist attacks thus becomes more crucial than ever. Already, experts are considering how the lessons learned from past disasters can be put into practice on the planes of tomorrow. Engineers and safety officials are also structuring tomorrow's planes so that people can get out in ninety seconds, should a crash occur.

In 1997 then NASA leader Daniel Goldin warned that the aviation industry needed to continue to make improvements in safety if it wanted to avoid a dramatic increase in the frequency of aircraft accidents. He said that the number of aircraft flying in the United States was projected to double, to about five hundred thousand aircraft, by 2010 and triple by 2020. If the current figure of 1.5 accidents for every million flights stayed the same, three times as many aircraft flying would translate to about one accident per week.

Along with the increased air traffic comes increased responsibility for the entire airline industry—as well as increased dangers for an already strained system. More people are needed in aviation to work in the towers, guard the gates, and fly the planes. Technology is sure to change the face of aviation more than anyone can predict, but flying will never lose its human factor. And though it seems impossible, all involved hope to see a day when planes travel without accidents or crimes.

Notes

Introduction: Safety Is Relative

1. Quoted in Curtis Prendergast, *The First Aviators*. Alexandria, VA: Time-Life Books, 1980, p. 58.

Chapter 1: Diverse Disasters

2. Michael Sivak and Michael J. Flannagan, "Flying and Driving After the September 11 Attacks," *American Scientist*. www.americanscientist.org.

3. *BBC News,* "Transcript: The Crew's Last Words," August 31, 2000. http://news.bbc.co.uk.

4. Quoted in *BBC News,* "Q&A: Concorde Crash," September 1, 2000. http://news.bbc.co.uk.

5. Al Haynes, "Eyewitness Report: United Flight 232," *AirDisaster.com.* www.airdisaster.com.

6. Haynes, *AirDisaster.com.*

7. Haynes, *AirDisaster.com.*

8. Quoted in Todd Curtis, "Plane Crash Involving 'Men in Black' Director Barry Sonnenfeld," *AirSafe.com.* www. airsafe.com.

9. Quoted in *CNN.com,* "Recovery Efforts to Resume Tuesday in Kenya Airways Jet Crash," January 31, 2000. www.cnn.com.

10. Quoted in Jason Carroll, "Crash Scene Already Scarred by September Attacks," *CNN.com,* November 12, 2001. www.cnn.com.

Chapter 2: The Rescue

11. *Panix.com,* "Transcript of Al Haynes's Talk at NASA/ Dryden." www.panix.com.

12. *Panix.com,* "Transcript of Al Haynes's Talk at NASA/ Dryden."

13. *Panix.com,* "Transcript of Al Haynes's Talk at NASA/ Dryden."

14. Haynes, *AirDisaster.com.*

15. Quoted in Macarthur Job and Matthew Tesch, *Air Disaster,* vol. 2. St. Paul, MN: Motorbooks International, 1996, p. 147.

16. Jim Gill, "The Gillam Plane Crash," Coast Guard Stories, *Jack's Joint.* www.jacksjoint.com.

Chapter 3: Causes of Airplane Crashes

17. *Aviation Safety Network,* "Accident Description, Flight 981." http://aviation-safety.net.

18. Quoted in Stephen Barlay, *The Final Call: Why Airline Disasters Continue to Happen.* New York: Pantheon, 1990, p. 405.

19. John Barry and Roger Charles, "Sea of Lies," *Newsweek,* July 13, 1992, p. 29.

20. Najaco Publishing, *The Indestructible Pilot.* www. najaco.com.

21. Quoted in David Grayson, *Terror in the Skies.* Secaucus, NJ: Citadel Press, 1988, pp. 169–70.

22. Quoted in Grayson, *Terror in the Skies,* p. 171.

23. Quoted in Grayson, *Terror in the Skies,* pp. 171–72.

24. Quoted in Craig R. Whitney, "Jetliner Carrying 258 to U.S. Crashes in Scottish Town," *New York Times,* December 21, 1988, International section.

Chapter 4: Specialized Investigations

25. *National Transportation Safety Board,* About the NTSB, "The Investigative Process." www.ntsb.gov.

26. Quoted in David Hanners, "Crash Will Put Investigators to the Test," *St. Paul Pioneer Press,* October 29, 2002. www.twincities.com.

27. Quoted in *BBC News,* Q&A: Concorde Crash."

28. Gary Katz, "Naming the Suspects," *CBC News Online.* http://cbc.ca.

Chapter 5: Safety Steps for the Future

29. Charles Perrow, *Normal Accidents: Living with High-Risk Technologies.* Princeton, NJ: Princeton University Press, 1999, p. 127.

30. Battelle Memorial Institute, "An Overview of the Scientific Literature Concerning Fatigue, Sleep, and the Circadian Cycle," *Allied Pilots Association.* www.alliedpilots.org.

31. Quoted in Jonathan D. Salant, "Controller Shortage on the Horizon?" *CBSNews.com,* June 18, 2002. www.cbsnews.com.

32. *National Transportation Safety Board,* "Safety Report: Survivability of Accidents Involving Part 121 U.S. Air Carrier Operations 1983 Through 2000." www.ntsb.gov.

33. David Evans, "Safety in Avionics: Time to Stop Fuel Tank Explosions," *Aviation Today.* www.aviationtoday.com.

34. Quoted in Dan Rupp, "An Interview with the NTSB," *Air Safety Online.* www.airsafetyonline.com.

35. William Langwiesche, "The Lessons of ValuJet 592," *Atlantic Monthly,* March 1998. www.theatlantic.com.

36. *Aircraft Owners and Pilots Association,* "Department of Homeland Security Advisory 03-019." www.aopa.org.

Glossary

aileron: A movable part of the airplane's wing that gives the plane stability when turning.

cabin: The pressurized portion inside the fuselage where passengers sit.

cockpit: The front section of the plane where pilots sit and control the aircraft.

drag: The natural forces of friction and resistance that retard an object's movement through the air.

elevator: A movable portion of the horizontal tail wing that causes the plane to gain or lose altitude.

Federal Aviation Administration (FAA): The U.S. government's regulatory body for the airline industry; it runs the nation's air traffic control system, makes and enforces safety and maintenance regulations, and assesses penalties.

fuselage: The center portion of the aircraft, designed to hold the cargo, passengers, and crew.

lift: The force created when air passes over and under a wing; pressure differences on the wing allow the aircraft to rise.

National Transportation Safety Board (NTSB): This federal agency does not make or enforce regulations but it is in charge of investigating car, airplane, train, and other crashes and passing recommendations on to other government agencies.

pressurization: The process of making the atmosphere inside the airplane nearly the same pressure as on the ground; this makes air travel at high altitudes possible.

rudder: A movable part of the plane's vertical tail wing that helps the plane turn.

thrust: The force an airplane engine generates to push the craft forward.

wing flap: A movable part on the airplane's wing that can increase or decrease lift.

For Further Reading

Books

Bill Adair, *The Mystery of Flight 427: Inside a Crash Investigation.* Washington, DC: Smithsonian Institution Press, 2002. Adair takes readers inside the investigation to show how true crash study works.

Larry Kusche, *The Disappearance of Flight 19.* New York: Harper & Row, 1980. Kusche attempts to resolve the mysterious disappearance of Flight 19 over the Bermuda Triangle.

Jere Longman, *Among the Heroes: United Flight 93 and the Passengers and Crew Who Fought Back.* New York: Harperperennial Library, 2003. An acclaimed *New York Times* writer gives a detailed and human account of the passengers who battled the terrorists on Flight 93 and kept it from crashing into a major landmark.

Piers Paul Read, *Alive.* New York: Avon, 1975. The compelling, tragic, and ultimately hopeful story of a rugby team that crashed in the Andes Mountains in 1973 and was not rescued until ten weeks later.

Websites

Federal Aviation Administration (www.faa.gov). Offers background on the FAA's regulatory and oversight role in U.S. aviation.

National Transportation Safety Board (www.ntsb.gov). Includes up-to-date accident reports, details of its investigative processes, tables showing accident statistics, and numerous other resources.

Works Consulted

Books

Stephen Barlay, *The Final Call: Why Airline Disasters Continue to Happen.* New York: Pantheon, 1990. The author shows how modern accidents often have precedents in earlier accidents.

James R. Chiles, *Inviting Disaster: Lessons from the Leading Edge of Technology.* New York: HarperBusiness, 2002. An entertaining summary of various disasters, including many airplane crashes.

David Grayson, *Terror in the Skies.* Secaucus, NJ: Citadel Press, 1988. Grayson explores some of the worst air disasters in history and gives strong, on-the-scenes explanations of what happened and why.

Macarthur Job and Matthew Tesch, *Air Disaster*, vol. 2. St. Paul, MN: Motorbooks International, 1996. Lively descriptions of diverse accidents.

Charles Perrow, *Normal Accidents: Living with High-Risk Technologies.* Princeton, NJ: Princeton University Press, 1999. Contains a revealing chapter on airline safety.

Curtis Prendergast, *The First Aviators.* Alexandria, VA: Time-Life Books, 1980. Recounts memorable characters and deeds.

Stanley Stewart, *Air Disasters.* London: Ian Allan, 1986. Somewhat technical but an excellent analysis of some of history's most famous crashes.

Periodicals

John Barry and Roger Charles, "Sea of Lies," *Newsweek*, July 13, 1992.

Craig R. Whitney, "Jetliner Carrying 258 to U.S. Crashes in Scottish Town," *New York Times*, December 21, 1988.

Internet Sources

Aircraft Owners and Pilots Association, "Department of Homeland Security Advisory 03-019." www.aopa.org.

Aviation Safety Network, "Accident Description, Flight 981." http://aviation-safety.net.

Battelle Memorial Institute, "An Overview of the Scientific Literature Concerning Fatigue, Sleep, and the Circadian Cycle," *Allied Pilots Association*. www.alliedpilots.org.

BBC News, "Q&A: Concorde Crash," September 1, 2000. http://news.bbc.co.uk.

———"Transcript: The Crew's Last Words," August 31, 2000. http://news.bbc.co.uk.

Jason Carroll, "Crash Scene Already Scarred by September Attacks," *CNN.com*, November 12, 2001. www.cnn.com.

CNN.com, "Federal Agencies Deny TWA Flight 800 Shot Down by Missile," November 8, 1996. www.cnn.com.

———"Recovery Efforts to Resume Tuesday in Kenya Airways Jet Crash," January 31, 2000. www.cnn.com.

Todd Curtis, "Plane Crash Involving 'Men in Black' Director Barry Sonnenfeld," *AirSafe.com*. www.airsafe.com.

David Evans, "Safety in Avionics: Time to Stop Fuel Tank Explosions," *Aviation Today*. www.aviationtoday.com.

Gidget Fuentes, "Mock Airplane Crash at Miramar Tests Military, Local Response," *North County Times*, August 23, 2001. www.nctimes.com.

Jim Gill, "The Gillam Plane Crash," Coast Guard Stories, *Jack's Joint*. www.jacksjoint.com.

Al Haynes, "Eyewitness Report: United Flight 232," *AirDisaster.com*. www.airdisaster.com.

David Hanners, "Crash Will Put Investigators to the Test," *St. Paul Pioneer Press*, October 29, 2002. www.twincities.com.

Gary Katz, "Naming the Suspects," *CBC News Online*. http://cbc.ca.

William Langwiesche, "The Lessons of ValuJet 592," *Atlantic Monthly*, March 1998. www.theatlantic.com.

Najaco Publishing, *The Indestructible Pilot*. www.najaco.com.

National Transportation Safety Board, About the NTSB, "The Investigative Process." www.ntsb.gov.

———"Safety Report: Survivability of Accidents Involving Part 121 U.S. Air Carrier Operations 1983 Through 2000." www.ntsb.gov.

Panix.com, "Transcript of Al Haynes's Talk at NASA/Dryden." www.panix.com.

Dan Rupp, "An Interview with the NTSB," *Air Safety Online*. www.airsafetyonline.com.

Jonathan D. Salant, "Controller Shortage on the Horizon?" *CBSNews.com*, June 18, 2002. www.cbsnews.com.

Michael Sivak and Michael J. Flannagan, "Flying and Driving After the September 11 Attacks," *American Scientist*. www.americanscientist.org.

Websites

AirDisaster.com (http://airdisaster.com). Includes survivor stories, statistics, accident reports, and editorials on airplane crashes.

Air Safety Online (www.airsafetyonline.com). An in-depth site that posts up-to-date air safety news and contains interviews with aviation officials and articles on airplane safety.

Aviation Safety Network (http://aviation-safety.net). With links to recent crashes, airplane crash reports, and pictures, this is a comprehensive site for studying airplane disasters.

Index

Picture Credits

About the Authors

Gordon D. Laws graduated with a Bachelor of Arts in English from Brigham Young University. He is the author of several short stories, numerous magazine articles, and the novel *My People*. Currently, he is a free-lance writer and editor. Lauren M. Laws graduated with a Bachelor of Arts in history from Brigham Young University. She is a researcher and records expert. In addition to this work, Gordon and Lauren collaborated on a number of titles in the Lucent Books Exploring Canada series. Gordon and Lauren live in Massachusetts with their son, Grant.